Why's he here?

It might not be him. There had to be more than one doctor named Oliver Cavendish. She changed into scrubs and headed to Resus. The red phone was ringing as she opened the door, and she picked it up and tried to focus.

"Yoxburgh Park Resus."

"Code red, eighteen-year-old male, motorbike versus car, open-book pelvis and lower-limb fractures, right-sided chest, possible clavicle, query head injury…"

"ETA?"

"Five minutes."

"Okay."

She hung up, put the message out on the public-address system and quickly beeped the anesthetist, Orthopedics, Radiography and Interventional Radiology.

She could hear the sound of the helicopter overhead, just as the door swished open behind her.

"Okay, what've we got?"

She turned at the familiar voice, her heart racing, and over her mask she met striking blue eyes she hadn't seen for nearly twenty years. Eyes that widened in shock.

"Emily?" His voice was incredulous, and for a second they stared at each other, and then the door swung open again, and she gave herself a mental shake and snapped back into doctor mode.

Dear Reader,

I love a reunion romance, with all the guilt and regrets and what-ifs that come with it, but what happens if it's eighteen years, three broken marriages and four children later?

Blending families isn't straightforward, and divorce leaves its scars on everyone. Can you ever go back that far and find a way to move forward? Emily and Oliver had a lot of heart-searching and forgiving to do, but they got there in the end.

I give them to you with my love. Be kind to them—they've earned it!

Caroline x

FINDING THEIR FOREVER FAMILY

CAROLINE ANDERSON

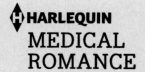

HARLEQUIN

MEDICAL ROMANCE

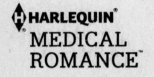

Recycling programs
for this product may
not exist in your area.

ISBN-13: 978-1-335-73774-8

Finding Their Forever Family

Copyright © 2023 by Caroline Anderson

For questions and comments about the quality of this book,
please contact us at CustomerService@Harlequin.com.

Harlequin Enterprises ULC
22 Adelaide St. West, 41st Floor
Toronto, Ontario M5H 4E3, Canada
www.Harlequin.com

Printed in U.S.A.

Caroline Anderson is a matriarch, writer, armchair gardener, unofficial tearoom researcher and eater of lovely cakes. Not necessarily in that order! What Caroline loves: Her family. Her friends. Reading. Writing contemporary love stories. Hearing from readers. Walks by the sea with coffee/ice cream/cake thrown in! Torrential rain. Sunshine in spring/autumn. What Caroline hates: Losing her pets. Fighting with her family. Cold weather. Hot weather. Computers. Clothes shopping. Caroline's plans: Keep smiling and writing!

Books by Caroline Anderson

Harlequin Medical Romance

Yoxburgh Park Hospital

Best Friend to Wife and Mother?
Their Meant-to-Be Baby
The Midwife's Longed-For Baby
Bound by Their Babies
Their Own Little Miracle
A Single Dad to Heal Her Heart
From Heartache to Forever
Tempted by the Single Mom
The Midwife's Miracle Twins

Healing Her Emergency Doc

Visit the Author Profile page at Harlequin.com for more titles.

Thanks to my daughters Sarah and Hannah and their families for the extensive opportunities to savor the agonies and ecstasies of parenting/stepparenting. So much material!
Love you all xxx.

CHAPTER ONE

SHE WAS LATE. Again.

She hurried in, racked with guilt and frustration as usual, and bumped straight into James Slater—clinical lead, department cheerleader and stickler for punctuality...

He quirked a brow and smiled wryly. 'Morning, Emily. What is it today?'

She rolled her eyes. 'Billy. I'm so sorry. He wouldn't put his shoes on.'

James chuckled. 'Take him to school without them. They only do it once. Anyway, I'm glad you're here. I'm putting you in Resus. I'm a bit tied up with meetings, and I need you to look after our new consultant.'

She felt her eyes widen. 'He needs babysitting?'

James laughed again. 'Hardly. He just needs to get to know the department. We were really lucky to get him. He's ex-LMTS.'

That surprised her. The London Major

Trauma System was world-class, and for a moment she wondered why on earth he'd chosen to come to Yoxburgh. Not that it wasn't a great hospital, but even so... Still, at least he'd be competent, unlike their last locum.

'OK. Give me a second to change. What's his name?'

'Oliver. Oliver Cavendish.'

She felt the shock all the way down to her toes, but there wasn't time to stop and think. Not that she knew *what* to think...

She nodded and walked away to the locker room, heart racing, her mind in turmoil.

Why's he here?

It might not be him. There had to be more than one doctor called Oliver Cavendish. She changed into scrubs, scraped back her hair into a messy bun and headed to Resus. The red phone was ringing as she opened the door, and she picked it up and tried to focus.

'Yoxburgh Park Resus.'

'Code Red, eighteen-year-old male, motorbike versus car, open book pelvis and lower limb fractures, right-sided chest, possible clavicle, query head injury...'

The list went on, and as she wrote it down, her heart started to race. If they got the young man in alive, it would be a miracle. Code Red was as bad as it got, and Oliver went clean out of her mind.

'ETA?'

'Five minutes. He's in the air.'

'OK.'

She hung up, put the message out on the Tannoy and fast bleeped the anaesthetist, orthopaedics, radiography, interventional radiology, and then booked a CT slot and checked the fridge for blood. Four units. Hopefully it'd be enough until they could cross-match.

She could hear the sound of the helicopter overhead as it came in to land, just as the door swished open behind her.

'OK, what've we got?'

She turned at the familiar voice, her heart racing, and over her mask she met striking blue eyes she hadn't seen for nearly twenty years. Eyes that widened in shock.

'Emily?' His voice was incredulous, and for a second they stared at each other, and then the door swung open again as more people came in, and she gave herself a mental shake and snapped back into doctor mode.

'Right, we have a Code Red, eighteen-year-old male, motorbike versus car...' She reeled off the list of injuries as the other members of the team poured into the room, and Oliver stood there, his focus absolute.

His eyes met hers. 'OK, this is a complicated polytrauma by the sound of it. Do you mind if I lead? I've done a lot of these.'

'No, not at all. Do you want me to go and meet them and you can brief?'

'Sure.'

She ran out to meet the casualty, and as they wheeled him into the now crowded Resus, she was wondering how on earth he was still alive. Not only alive, but conscious enough to moan and mumble something she couldn't understand.

'It's OK, Jack. We've got you,' she told him gently, and grabbed a corner of the sheet. 'On three. One, two, slide—'

'Right, what do we know?' Oliver asked, taking over.

The air ambulance doctor rattled off the list of injuries from top to toe, detailed the treatment he'd received so far, including a pelvic binder, and then told them the family were on the way. As she finished, he nodded and moved straight to the patient's head and bent over him.

'Hi, Jack. I'm Oliver. I'm one of the doctors here. Can you tell me where you hurt?'

The boy's eyes rolled a little, and he mumbled something incoherent.

'Jack, can you squeeze my hand?' he asked,

then shook his head. 'He's not obeying commands. We need to send him off to sleep so we can get a proper look at him. Do we have an anaesthetist here?'

'Yup, I'm on it,' Peter said, and while he put Jack under and intubated him, the rest of the team were assembling the equipment they'd need, putting up drips, warming blood, cutting off the rest of his clothes to reveal his injuries to Oliver.

'OK, he's got reduced air entry on the right, so let's get a chest drain in. Emily, can you do that, please? And there's something very wrong with that pelvis. We need to scan him as soon as we can, but we need to get him stable and I don't think we're quite there yet. Let's get the chest drain in and a catheter to check his bladder and see where we are then. Can you start rapid transfusion, please, and take bloods for group and save? And that left foot's very pale.'

The orthopaedic consultant was already looking at it. 'Yeah, it's the ankle. I'll reduce the fracture now,' Dan said, and while he and a nurse did that, Emily prepped for the chest drain, aware of Oliver's every move, every breath, every word, not sure if the surge in her heart rate was because of him or because of their patient or both. Either would have been enough, but Oliver Cavendish could wait. Had to wait. It had been almost twenty years. Another hour or two wouldn't matter.

Jack was their priority, and until he was stable, scanned and shipped off to whoever was going to tackle his complicated injuries first, her feelings were on the back burner. As for Oliver's feelings—well, she had no idea what they were. Her own were enough to deal with and she wasn't sure what they were, either.

She shut her eyes for a moment, took a steadying breath and inserted the chest drain...

It took nearly an hour, but finally Oliver felt confident that Jack was reasonably stable, or at least for now. 'Right, I think we need to get him to CT. Are they ready for us?'

'Yes. I've asked them to hold it.'

'Good.' He looked up, catching Emily's eyes briefly before he dragged his own away and scanned the team. 'Do we all think he's stable enough to go? Anyone got any concerns?'

'Well, he's not great, but I think he's as good as we can get him without more information,' Peter said quietly, echoing all their thoughts.

'OK, I'll go with him. Peter, can you come, too, please? And, Emily, could you talk to the family?'

'Sure.'

And heaven help them if Jack died.

He's only a year older than Charlie...

They wheeled him down to CT, then stood side by side, watching the images appear. They weren't pretty, and not for the first time he wondered if his first case was going to survive.

He had multiple fractures—his pelvis, the right side of his ribcage, his left ankle and right wrist were all fractured, but there were no spinal or skull fractures, and at least his aorta was intact. That had been a worry from the start.

As had the quality of the team. Because the last thing he'd needed was an unskilled crew on a case like this, but to his immense relief they seemed to work well together and know what they were doing. And Emily—so calm and competent, she'd quietly got on with it, and he was pretty sure if he hadn't been there, she would have coped fine alone. Impressive. And disturbing.

Why's she here?

He refocused on the screen and frowned. 'Wait—can we have another look at his heart, please?'

And there it was.

'Pericardial effusion. Damn. Right, can you get Dan Wheeler to look at the images immediately, please, and let's get him back. He might need that drained. Thank you.'

They got back to Resus and found the orthopaedic surgeon studying the images with Joe Baker, the interventional radiologist, while Emily was on the phone trying to book a theatre.

'He's a mess,' Dan told him, and he dragged his eyes off Emily and concentrated on Dan's words. 'We need to sort this before he bleeds out. I'm going to need IR to deal with that, so Joe's coming in if the crossover surgical suite's available.'

'It's on standby for you,' Emily said, hanging up the phone. 'What are we doing about the pericardial effusion?'

'I'm not sure,' Oliver told them, glad to see that Emily had spotted it. 'How's he doing, Peter? Is he stable?'

'No,' Peter said, shaking his head. 'BP's dropped to eighty over fifty, heart rate's up to one thirty, and his jugulars are distended.'

'Tamponade,' he said, and looked around. 'Right, let's get some imaging of this. I'm going to do a pericardial tap.'

'The trolley's ready,' Emily said, moving it into position with everything laid out for him, and he picked up the long needle and took a steadying breath, grateful that she was on the ball.

Under image guidance he advanced the long needle up through Jack's diaphragm and into the blood-filled space between his heart and the pericardial membrane, slid a fine tube up through the needle and withdrew it, then took off thirty-five mils of blood.

And waited.

'Come on, Jack, you can do this,' Oliver muttered, and then after a few heart-stopping seconds, he started to respond.

'BP's up to one ten over sixty, heart rate's down to eighty-six,' Peter said, and he felt the tension in the room ease a fraction.

Not his. Not yet.

'So far so good,' he murmured, and checked the images again. Better. He withdrew the fine tube, watched the monitor for a few more moments, then turned to Peter.

'How's he looking now?'

'Good. Better. The jugulars are back to normal.'

He nodded, relieved, and turned to Dan.

'Happy to take over?' he said, and Dan nodded.

'Absolutely. I want to get him sorted asap.'

Oliver thanked them as they wheeled him out, Peter going with them, then looked around at the rest of the team, feeling the tension drain out of them all as the responsibility for young Jack was passed on up the line.

'Thank you. That was great teamwork. He's not out of the woods yet, but we've given him a fighting chance, so thank you all for that. It's good to know I've got a strong team with me.'

And then he turned his head and met the soft, beautiful but very guarded grey eyes that he knew so well. 'We need to talk to the parents. What have you told them?'

'Only what we knew before the CT. They're in the family room.'

'Come with me?'

'Sure.'

They were distraught, but sobbed with relief when they were told he was still alive, stable and on his way to Theatre.

'We'll keep you in the loop,' he promised. 'When he comes out of Theatre, they'll give you a call and update you on his condition, but he'll be going to ICU while they monitor his progress, probably for a few days, and then it'll be a long, slow job, I'm afraid. He's still not out of the woods by any means, but he's very lucky to be alive and at least now he stands a chance.'

'How long will the operation take?' his father asked.

'I don't know. It could be several hours. It's tricky surgery.'

'And will it work? Will he walk again? And what about his heart?' his mother asked, her eyes wide with fear and worry. He could understand that. If this had happened to Charlie...

'I would very much hope so, but his pelvis is quite badly broken and it'll take a lot of skill to sort it out. In the meantime his heart seems to have recovered from the bleed, so that's one hurdle crossed.'

'Is the surgeon any good?' his father asked, and before Oliver could open his mouth, Emily jumped in.

'He's excellent. If that was my son, I'd want Mr Wheeler working on him. He really is in very good hands.'

He saw the tension drain out of them, and after answering a few more questions, they showed them the way out to the main café where they could wait for news.

Oliver watched them go, her words echoing in his head.

If that was my son... Did she have a son, too?

'Emily, have you got time for a debrief?'

Had she? She didn't know. Maybe, maybe not, but now the clinical pressure was off, the emotional pressure was well and truly on, and her heart kicked behind her ribs.

'Sure.' Damn, why did her voice sound breathy and ridiculous? 'Of course,' she said, injecting a bit more oomph into it. Better...

'Right. First stop, coffee.'

She stared at him, stunned. 'Seriously?'

'Absolutely dead seriously. I've been here since six and I haven't had breakfast, and if I'm not going to fall over, I need something fast and filling right now. So where do we go?'

She was about to say the staff-room, but the coffee was vile, the biscuit tin would be empty, and anyway, it wouldn't tick the 'fast and filling' box.

'Park Café. We can go round the side.'

She turned on her heel and headed out through a staff door, and he followed her, before reaching past her to push the door open, bringing his body so close to her that the remembered scent of him filled her nostrils and made her ache with longing.

He fell into step beside her. 'Thanks for your help this morning. You're good,' he said, and she shot him a look, desperately trying to ignore the leap in her pulse at his nearness.

'You don't have to sound surprised.'

The low chuckle rippled all the way down her spine. 'I'm not. I'm just being honest. I was glad to have you in there. They're a sound team. I was very relieved about that.'

She found a smile from somewhere. 'Yes, it wasn't exactly finding your feet gently, was it?'

That chuckle again. 'Not exactly. And there I thought I might get bored doing a nice quiet little job, in a pretty seaside town where nothing much happens...'

Emily laughed at that. 'Quiet? I wish. You do realize this is a major hospital?'

'It's beginning to dawn on me,' he said, his grin wry and achingly familiar.

'So how come you're here?' she asked, partly because she was desperately curious and partly to fill the silence. 'Why on earth would you leave an LMTS hospital to come to Yoxburgh? Because it doesn't sound like you were looking for a quiet life.'

'Family reasons,' he said, without elaborating, and then added, 'and I could ask why you're here.'

'You probably could,' she said, and deliberately didn't answer it, just walked into the café and joined the queue. Better the silence than getting into that one...

He ordered a large cappuccino, picked up an egg and cress sandwich and a banana, and watched while she dithered over the pastries, then chose a chicken salad sandwich, a yogurt and a fruit tea.

'That's not like you.'

'Actually it is—well, it is now. I have a bit more respect for my body than I did twenty years ago, and it looks like you have, too.'

'Touché,' he murmured, then his mouth kicked up in a smile, and her world tilted sideways. This was such a bad idea...

'In or out?' she asked, looking hastily away.

'Out. It's a gorgeous day.'

He picked up the tray and headed through the doors, and she followed him to an empty table for two. It was set against the wall in the sun, and there was no alternative but to sit opposite each other.

He ripped open his sandwich and took a huge bite, and for a moment neither of them said anything. He, she guessed, because he couldn't talk with his mouth full, and she because she was too busy searching for all the changes the last however long had etched on his face.

That and wondering what the 'family reasons' were...

He glanced up, and she peeled open her yogurt, stuck the spoon in it and looked up again, finally meeting his eyes. Thoughtful, questioning eyes.

'I can't believe you're here,' he said softly after a pause that stopped the breath in her throat, and she looked down again and fiddled with the yogurt, stirring it mindlessly.

'Ditto.' She looked up again, studying him as he took another huge bite. The new lines around the eyes, the creases at each side of his mouth, the touch of grey threaded through his dark hair at the temples.

And then her curiosity got the better of her. 'So what have you been up to for the last— what is it? Eighteen years?'

'Something like that.' He gave a rueful huff of laughter and turned his attention to his coffee, avoiding her eyes, as she'd just avoided his, then when she'd given up expecting him to answer, he gave a shrug and smiled, but it didn't reach his eyes.

'Working too hard, trying to decide what I wanted to do—you know how it goes, but the move back to a major London hospital was the decider.'

'I'm surprised it took you so long to work out. You always were an adrenaline junkie.'

'And you weren't, so why are you here doing this?'

She looked away from those suddenly searching eyes. 'I've changed. I guess we both have. We've been doctors almost half our lives, seen all manner of things that most people never get exposed to. It would be weird if it hadn't changed us.'

He nodded slowly. 'Yes, I guess it would. Are you going to eat that yogurt or just play with it, because we really need to get back.'

And just like that, he shut it down.

He swallowed the last bite of his sandwich as she scraped out the pot, then finished his coffee and looked at her. 'Ready?'

'Sure.'

She drained her cup and stood up, stuffing her sandwich into her scrubs pocket. 'Lunch,' she said, and he rolled his eyes.

'If we get that lucky.'

They didn't. So much for his nice quiet little job...

The rest of the day was chaos, with ambulances queueing up outside, waiting to offload as they dealt with a deluge of patients with chest or abdominal pain, head injuries, nasty fractures and all the rest, not to mention the never-ending supply of walking wounded, most of whom could have been seen by their family doctors.

As for lunch, that was never going to happen. Still, at least he wasn't bored, and it was a good introduction to the efficiency of the department, the skill sets of the various team members and the lack of ego amongst the doctors in particular.

He'd met some egos in his time, especially in the early days, and it was a relief to see that everyone here was treated with respect regardless of their grade or position. He was all for that. He knew just how hard it was to forge a career in medicine, knew the toll that working in trauma and emergency medicine took on you, the drain on your reserves, the destruction of your personal life brick by brick until there was nothing left.

He knew all about that one from bitter experience. And if you felt unsupported at work, that was the last straw, and it was the reason so many good doctors and nurses walked away.

But not Emily.

Emily was still there, working alongside him on the more complex cases, independently the rest of the time but always in the background—and it was getting to him.

He'd never in a million years imagined he'd end up working with her, not least because eighteen years ago she was aiming for surgery, and now she was working in the ED. Why had she changed her mind? And where had she been? What had she done with her life? Was she married? Did she have children? Was she happy?

That most of all. He hoped so. He was, but it was a qualified happiness, underpinned by a lot of regret and remorse. Not to mention failure.

He looked across the central desk and saw her, her face lit up with laughter as she shared a joke with a colleague, and it hit him like a punch to the gut.

No. He wasn't going there. Not again. His heart had been broken enough times without him throwing it under the bus for the hell of it, and that particular bus had run him over before.

'You OK? Has Emily been looking after you?'

He turned his head and conjured up a smile for James.

'Yes, thanks. She's been great.'

His new boss smiled wryly. 'She is great. It's a pity she can't work full time, but her children come first and it's a bit of a juggling act. She's a very good doctor, though, and we're glad to have her. She's an asset to the department.'

So she *was* a mother, working part-time,

presumably with a husband and family around her. He told himself he was happy for her, and he was, but it just underlined how much he'd lost over the years.

Starting with her...

He walked round to the other side of the desk just as she reached it.

'I've had some news about Jack,' he told her. 'His pelvis came together better than expected, and they've taken him up to ICU. They'll keep him under for a day or so, sort out some of his other issues, and then slowly ease off on the drugs and see where we are, but it's looking good and his heart seems OK now, so that's a relief. I thought you'd like to know.'

Her smile was genuine and heartfelt. 'Absolutely. I've been really worried about him. His parents will be so relieved.'

'They are, apparently. They sent their thanks to the team and said everyone's been brilliant.'

'Oh, that's nice. It's good to feel appreciated. Right, I'm off. See you tomorrow,' she murmured, and he dug out a smile.

'Yeah. Thanks for holding my hand today.'

'You're welcome. Sorry, I have to go.'

Presumably to pick up her children from school. Interesting—and none of his business. She hurried away, and he turned back to James. 'So, what's next?'

* * *

She couldn't believe he was back in her life.

And why, oh, why did he still have to be so ridiculously gorgeous? Why couldn't he have got saggy and paunchy and lost his hair or something? Instead he was slimmer, more toned, and age had done his insanely good looks no harm at all. If anything it had honed them—that and his charismatic manner, the way he made a point of thanking his team, the quirk of his lips when he smiled...

He was just too darned perfect.

And she needed to stop torturing herself. She wasn't in the market for a relationship, particularly not one which had already failed nearly two decades ago.

No, not failed. Just been put on hold when he'd gone to Chicago, and then crashed and burned, taking her heart and her trust with it. Should she have gone? She'd kicked herself for not going at the time, and maybe she'd been wrong to let him go without a fight. How different would their lives have been?

Too late to worry about that now...

She parked the car, walked to the school gate and waited for the children to come out. There were a couple of older women there, standing chatting, and one looked vaguely familiar, but she couldn't place her. An ex-patient? Maybe, although she didn't think so. She hadn't seen her here before, certainly, but then she was often a bit late.

The children ran out, Phoebe straight for her, Billy detouring to chase another boy, then eventually ambling over to her before being sent back for his jumper.

'So what did you do today?' she asked Phoebe, scooping her up for a cuddle. It was an unnecessary question, as she was splattered with paint from her hair to her shoes, but Phoebe told her, moment by moment, and she nodded and smiled and felt relieved that her little daughter was so happy in school.

By the time Billy re-emerged, his jumper trailing on the ground behind him, almost everyone had gone, and she took them home, sent them out to the garden with a drink and opened the fridge.

'Can we have pasta?' Billy asked, sticking his head back into the kitchen, and she rolled her eyes.

'Again?'

'I like pasta.'

'I'll see.'

He went, not looking convinced, and she stared at the fridge again. There was a chicken, which wouldn't keep, so she pressure-cooked it, stripped some of the meat off and threw it in with a bowl of pasta and pesto, added some peas and sweet corn, and called the children in.

'Yay, pasta!' Billy said, and Phoebe pulled a face.

'We *always* have pasta,' she grumbled, but frankly putting anything on the table that was edible was a miracle, the way she felt today.

Confused didn't even scrape the surface.

'We'll have something else tomorrow,' she promised, and gave the ever-hungry Billy another dollop.

'So how was your first day?'

He straightened up from fussing the dog and gave his mother a wry smile.

'Interesting. Pretty full-on, really, but good. We had a boy just a year older than Charlie— his motorbike hit a car head-on. It was pretty messy, and I had no idea how everyone there would cope. Back in London I wouldn't have worried, everyone knew what to do, but actually it was brilliant. They're a good team, and he's doing OK, so that's good.'

She eyed him thoughtfully. 'And?'

'Well, it was touch and go and just a bit close to home.'

'I'm sure, but it's not what I'm talking about.'

He laughed. He'd never been able to hide

anything from his mother, and he gave up try-ing. 'Emily's there. She was one of the team.'

Her brows creased in a thoughtful frown. 'Emily Harrison?'

'She's Emily West now. She's a senior spe-cialty registrar—what? Why are you looking at me like that?'

'Does she have children?'

'I think so, maybe.'

'A boy and a girl?'

He raised his hands, confused. 'I don't know. I have no idea. Why?'

'Because I saw someone today after school who looked rather like her, but I thought I must be imagining it. She had a little girl with blonde hair—about four, I suppose, and a boy of about five or six called Billy, with grubby knees and the cheekiest smile you've ever seen.'

That made him laugh, but his breath caught and deep inside there was a tiny pang of regret for what might have been. If they'd stayed to-gether, those could have been their children, his and hers. He stamped on that before it had time to take root, and made his voice deliber-ately light. 'I have no idea. I don't know how old they are or what they're called. More to the point, how was Amelie's first day? She seems to have enjoyed it, from what she said just now when I went up.'

'I think she's fine. She certainly didn't seem unhappy, but it's early days. But you know her, Oliver. She makes friends really easily.'

'She loses them again pretty quickly, as well,' he reminded her with a wry smile, and she nodded.

'She'll learn,' his mother said soothingly, and slid a cup of tea across the island to him. 'Are you hungry?'

He gave a slightly hollow laugh. 'You could say that. I had a sandwich about eleven thirty, and a banana at some point, and probably way too much coffee. What are you offering? Because I could eat a horse.'

'Sorry, no horses, but I made a fish pie.'

His stomach growled, and he smiled wearily. 'That sounds amazing. Bring it on...'

She didn't let it rest, of course.

She wanted every last detail of his day, every last detail of how Emily looked, how she'd sounded, how he felt about her being there.

That was the tough one to answer, because he really didn't know. It had certainly made it harder to settle in and focus, because she'd been all he could think about, all he could hear, all he could see. Everywhere he turned, she was there, or there was the echo of her laugh, the soft murmur of her voice soothing a patient, talking to a relative, comforting a frightened child.

And then, as if the day itself hadn't been enough to contend with, that night he dreamt about her and woke up with a racing heart and a body that was more than ready to welcome her back into his bed.

This was going to be impossible to ignore. *She* was going to be impossible to ignore. And seeing her again had brought a whole lot of memories flooding back. Memories of her in his arms. Memories of them laughing together at something ridiculous, laughing at each other and themselves. Fighting about silly things, and then making up…

Damn. He rolled onto his back, stared up at the ceiling and wondered if moving here had been the biggest mistake of his life.

No. That prize had to go to his decision to go to America, and then to try and forget her in the arms of another woman, and look how well that had turned out.

Except it had given him Charlie, and for that he'd always be grateful. He looked at his watch. Two fifteen. It would be nine fifteen in Boston. He'd still be up.

He sat up, dragged a hand through his hair, reached for his phone and called his son.

CHAPTER TWO

THE ED WAS busy as usual.

For once that was a good thing, because if she wasn't busy, she'd have time to think about him, and she really, really didn't want to do that. The last thing she needed was to get sucked into that again. It had taken her years to get over him, and yesterday had made her realize she wasn't really over him at all. She'd just learned to live with it in the background.

Seeing him again had brought all those old feelings rushing back, the good ones as well as the bad, and it wasn't conducive to sleep, apparently. She'd had three, maybe four hours, in fits and starts, and in the end she'd got up and busied herself in the kitchen, making tonight's meal out of the leftover chicken and freezing the rest for some point in the future.

Then she'd curled up in the sitting room for a few quiet minutes, staring out over the garden as the sun came up and sparkled on the dewy grass, before she'd showered and dressed. And dithered over make-up.

To wear, or not to wear?

She'd scowled crossly at herself in the bathroom mirror, put on her usual flick of mascara, a touch of lippy and a streak of concealer to hide the shadows under her eyes, and got the children ready for school.

They were surprisingly cooperative for once, which meant she was early, and James opened his mouth to comment and was firmly shut down with a challenging look.

His lips twitched. 'I never said a word,' he murmured, but her relief was short-lived because he followed it up with, 'Can I ask you to work with Oliver again? Just until he's found his feet?'

He'd looked pretty sure on his feet yesterday, but she agreed, wishing she could say no but knowing it would demand a whole bunch of explanations she wasn't inclined to give right then. Mostly because she had no idea what to say.

It didn't matter. James just nodded and strode off to speak to Tom Stryker, leaving her to deal with her tangled emotions as she worked side by side with Oliver on one case after another.

And then at half past one it went weirdly quiet.

For the first time she could remember, they had no urgent cases that weren't already under control, leaving her to twiddle her thumbs.

She stuck her head into Minors and found everything there running smoothly and under control, so she was redundant. It wouldn't last, she knew that, but as she walked back into Majors, she all but fell over Oliver.

'Where is everyone?' he asked, looking puzzled.

'Who knows? It's like everyone's left town.'

He chuckled. 'It was a busy morning. Maybe they've got it out of their system.' He glanced at his phone. 'Quick coffee in the park?'

No! Not again. Too dangerous…

'That's asking for chaos.'

'I'll take the risk. You can fill me in on everything I need to know about everybody.'

Really? She shrugged and gave in. 'OK, but you're buying, and I'm hungry today—I need lunch. Just so you know.'

They found a bench under a tree, and sat down with their coffees and sandwiches, pagers at the ready because it really couldn't last.

'So, what do you want to know about us?' she asked, just to break the silence that was echoing with memories she'd really rather have forgotten.

He shot her an odd look, as if he knew what she was thinking, then followed up with a crooked smile.

'I don't know. You tell me. I'm sure I'll work it all out, unless there's anything really out there that you think I should know in advance?'

She shook her head, partly to clear it, and stuck to the script. 'Not much. Andy Gallagher's part-time. He had a benign meningioma removed a few years back and wanted a better work–life balance, and Tom Stryker's got retinitis pigmentosa and his peripheral vision's a bit dodgy, so if you end up working with him, you need to bear that in mind. Otherwise, no. Sam's an ex-army medic like Ryan, and he's pretty gung ho, but he's very good, so is Ryan, and James is just great. The junior doctors are by and large OK, there's the odd one that needs watching, but all the nurses are lovely.'

He nodded slowly. 'OK. That's good to know.'

He searched her eyes, and she had to look away because there was something in his steady gaze that made her heart race and her breath catch.

'And you?' he asked, his voice low and slightly husky. 'What do I need to know about you?'

Nothing...

'There's not much you don't know. I'm still just me,' she said lightly. 'I've been here for a year and a half, initially covering Tom's wife, Laura, on her maternity leave, and when she decided not to come back, I stayed on in the post and took on a bit more. Anyway, enough of us all,' she said, changing tack. 'What do we need to know about *you*?'

He gave a soft laugh, but his eyes changed, as if he was shielding himself somehow. Why? Although she could talk...

'I'm still just me,' he echoed with a slight smile. 'I've been working in London, as you know, and it was time for a move.'

She wondered why. He'd said family reasons yesterday but didn't add any more, so she probed a little deeper.

'So when did you come back from America? The last thing I knew you were in Chicago and you were getting married and having a baby.'

And breaking my heart in the process...

He looked away. 'Yeah. That didn't last too long. Just long enough to move back to the UK, have Charlie, and for Sue to meet someone else. They're living back in the States now—been there for four years, since he was thirteen, and I hardly see him.'

Wow. That shocked her. 'You couldn't have gone back there so you could be near him?'

He shook his head. 'No. I was married again by the time they moved back, we had a child, and Kath was working a lot in Europe, so it wasn't practical.'

'You've got another child?' she said, feeling a curious pang of something she didn't want to analyse, and he nodded.

'Yes. Amelie. She's five and a half now, and she's just a bundle of mischief.'

His eyes softened, and she could see the love in them. She'd bet her life he was a wonderful father, and he must miss Charlie so much. How would she feel if that was Billy?

Gutted.

'So tell me about you,' he went on, switching the subject back to her. 'James said you only work part-time, and Mum said she thought she saw you outside the school yesterday, so I gather you've got children, too.'

'It was *her*!' she said, the penny dropping at last. 'I was sure it was someone I knew, but I couldn't place her. So how come she was there?'

'She helps with the school run,' he said, but there was something else he didn't say.

She had no idea what it was, but now wasn't the time because he was moving on, or rather back, to the subject of her children.

'She told me you had a little girl with blonde hair and a boy called Billy with the cheekiest smile?' he added, which made her laugh.

'That sounds about right.'

'Well, come on, then, tell me more.'

She wasn't sure she wanted to—it seemed too personal, but what could it hurt? It wasn't like she was ashamed of them or anything, and she could hardly hide them if his child was at the same school, but he didn't need the whole sorry saga.

She gave a little shrug. 'There's not much more to tell. Phoebe's four and a half, and Billy's just six.'

'And their father? What does he do?'

Trust him to get to that.

'He's an accountant, but we're divorced,' she said reluctantly, looking away. 'He has our two every other weekend, which is good because I then work two long days, which gives me a chance to make up some hours. Otherwise, I wouldn't be able to afford the house.'

'Doesn't he pay maintenance?'

'Yes, of course he does, but I wanted a house in a good school catchment area, so I have to pay the premium for that. It's only a modest little house, but it's big enough for us and it's going to be mine one day, but it does mean I have to work more than I want to while they're so young.'

'You couldn't have stayed in the family home?'

'No, because it was in Nottingham, and he moved down here, so when this job came up I followed for the sake of the kids. It's just a bit tough at the moment, but I'll get there, one day.'

He stared at her for a long moment, then shook his head.

'I'm sorry.'

'What for? It's not your fault. You haven't done anything wrong—well, apart from dumping me nineteen years ago to follow your dream.'

His mouth twisted into a bitter little smile. 'I didn't exactly dump you. I asked you to come.'

'And I couldn't, you knew that, and you were going for a year and coming back. That was the plan. You going off with someone else wasn't *exactly* on the cards.'

He frowned and looked away. 'No. No, it wasn't. And I am sorry about that.'

'Is that it? "I'm sorry" is supposed to make it all OK? Is that what your letter was all about?'

'Of course not. I'm not that stupid. I didn't know what else to do, how to tell you, and you didn't reply.'

She gave a tiny humourless laugh. 'What did you expect? Congratulations? A wedding present? There was nothing to say, Oliver. Sue was pregnant, you were getting married. End of.'

He was looking down, peeling a crust off his sandwich and throwing it to the robin who was eyeing them patiently, his face sombre. 'I've often wondered what happened to you.'

'You could have asked me. I wouldn't have been difficult to find if you'd tried.'

'No, you wouldn't, but I didn't try.'

'Why?'

He shrugged. 'I didn't think it was fair. I thought I'd done enough damage, and I had nothing to offer you, and it wouldn't have changed anything, except to make it harder. Then when I did eventually look, I couldn't find you. I thought you were probably married, but I'm surprised you changed your name.'

'I did it for the children,' she said simply. 'I didn't want them having the confusion of a different last name to me, so it made sense.'

'Yes, I can understand that—oh, here we go…'

He picked up his pager and sighed, just as

hers went off, and as they scooped up the remains of their sandwiches and their coffees, they could hear the sound of the helicopter overhead.

'So much for my quiet life,' he said drily, and they headed back to Resus in a slightly awkward silence.

She left barely in time to collect the children from after-school club, and found Phoebe in tears because she'd lost her teddy and Billy with a plaster on his knee after a fall in the playground. He started to limp as soon as he saw her, but she wasn't fooled, just rumpled his hair and gave him a hug, scooped Phoebe up and headed for the car.

'I can't go home without him,' Phoebe sobbed. 'What if Mrs Ellis can't find him?'

'Don't worry about Mister Ted,' she soothed. 'He'll turn up. I'll bet when you get to school tomorrow, he'll be waiting for you.' And heaven help us if he's not...

'What if he's lost for ever?' she asked, and started to sob again as Emily strapped her in.

'I'm sure he's not,' she said, crossing her fingers and sliding behind the wheel. 'He'll turn up, you'll see. So what did you both do today?'

'We've got a new girl in our class this week,'

Billy told her. 'She's called Emily. Or I think she is, but she said it funny.'

That caught her attention. 'Amelie?' she suggested, with a little hitch in her heart.

'Yes. Why doesn't she just say Emily?'

'Perhaps because she's actually called Amelie. It's a French name, and someone at work has a daughter called Amelie who's just started at school near here, so maybe it's her.'

'Oh.'

She watched him in the rearview mirror, working that one out while she did the same thing. Was it purely coincidence that their names were so alike? Must be. And she really shouldn't start reading things into that...

'Can we have pasta?' he asked, moving on to his favourite subject, and she rolled her eyes.

'No. Not again.'

'I want chicken pie,' Phoebe said.

'I hate chicken pie!'

'Well, I *like* chicken pie,' Phoebe said, 'and I lost my teddy and it's my turn to choose. I want pie.'

'Well, isn't that lucky, because it's what we're having,' Emily told them, turning onto her drive with an inward sigh of relief. 'Come on, let's get that knee cleaned up and then we'll go in the garden. I need to cut the grass before we can eat.'

* * *

She was single.

So was he.

And he had no idea how he felt about that. Wary? Nervous? Excited?

No! He wasn't going there, not ever again, and certainly not with Emily! Not that she'd have him, judging by what she'd said today.

Smart woman. He wasn't a good husband. Couldn't be, could he, or two women wouldn't have left him for someone else. Although Sue's justification was a bit different, but Kath's wasn't. She'd found someone who'd be there when she was able to be at home, not someone who might well be on duty for the two days she was back in the country before her own better-paid high-flying job took her away again.

She'd wanted a house husband, but he hadn't realized that until it was too late, and there was no way he'd been going to give up his career to sit at home and wait for her, any more than she'd have done it for him. And that was the kiss of death for their marriage. Not that it had been great to start with...

No. Never again, not with Emily, not with anyone. He had his mother on tap if he wanted adult company, Amelie any time he needed a cuddle, and Charlie was on the end of the phone. Failing that, there was the dog who was always up for a hug and a bit of affection, and absolutely never judged him.

What more could any man want?

A friend?

He had friends. Good friends. Although he'd lost contact with most of them over the years, like he'd lost contact with Em. Work pressure, lifestyle differences, geography— there weren't many people left who he could call a real friend, but a part of him yearned to be friends with Emily again.

Not lovers. That was messy and would open all sorts of wounds, but...friends? She'd said her ex had the children every other weekend and she worked then, but not for forty-eight hours straight. Maybe he should take her out for dinner?

Except he'd have to ask his mother to baby-sit, and she did enough already—and besides, her matchmaking antennae would be having a field day.

Best not. Even if it would be nice...

Mrs Ellis and Mister Ted were waiting for Phoebe when they arrived, and Phoebe grabbed him and hugged him tight.

'I told you he'd be all right,' Emily said, and Phoebe ran off smiling. Billy was long gone, playing with his friends in the playground, and as she walked towards the gate, she spotted Oliver's mother, with a small shaggy dog and a little girl.

Amelie. Had to be. She was the spitting image of Oliver, and her heart thumped. Long dark hair scraped back into a bouncy ponytail, pink dungarees and a unicorn on her T-shirt peeping over the top of the bib, she was the picture of health and happiness, and Emily stood rooted to the spot.

The woman kissed her goodbye and then turned and greeted Emily with a wide smile and open arms.

'Emily, it *is* you! How lovely to see you again!'

'Hello, Elizabeth!' she said, and found herself engulfed in a warm motherly hug that brought tears to her eyes. She'd loved his mother, and it seemed it was mutual.

Elizabeth let go of her after a long moment, stood back and smiled. 'Oh, it's so good to see you again. Are you off to work?'

She nodded. 'Yup, afraid so.'

'Oh, that's a shame. It would be lovely to catch up with you. How would you feel about a play date after school one day? You can come round to ours.'

Ours? Her heart skipped a beat. They'd been living in Hampshire when she'd known them, so they must have moved up here. Or did she mean Oliver's home? And what about his wife? It was a minefield, and she tiptoed her way out of it.

'Why don't you come to mine?' she suggested, opting for safety, and Elizabeth pounced on it.

'Oh, that would be lovely! How nice. We can take it in turns. How about after school today?'

She hesitated, mentally ran an eye over her house and decided it would do, then nodded. 'OK. Actually, that would be great. I'll meet you here?'

'Perfect. Have a good day. I'll see you later.' Elizabeth kissed her cheek, and Emily walked away with a whole bunch of mixed feelings and tumbling emotions.

Was it wise to get reeled in? To forge a relationship with his mother at the same time as trying to keep him at arm's length to preserve her heart and her sanity?

Too late now; she'd agreed, but if the children didn't get on, she could always use that as an excuse to avoid it happening again, and it would give her a chance to find out a little more about him and his life now.

'My mother says you're going on a play date.'

Emily laughed at him and shook her head.

'That sounds so weird. She's coming round to mine with Amelie after school. It's not very exciting.'

'She's looking forward to it,' he said, searching her face and wondering whether she was. Possibly not, judging by the guarded look in her eyes, and he certainly wasn't thrilled.

'You could always put her off if you don't want to do it,' he added hopefully after a moment, but she shook her head.

'No, it's lovely to see her again. I was very fond of her.'

'Yes, it's mutual,' he said wryly. 'I'm not sure she's ever really forgiven me for breaking up with you.'

Which made at least two of them, if not three. He certainly hadn't forgiven himself, and from what she'd said yesterday, Emily might not have, either.

Too late now. The damage was done, and he wasn't going there again, but he wondered how much his mother would tell Emily about him. Nothing, hopefully, but it was probably a vain hope.

'So how come she's doing the school run?' Emily asked, ignoring his last comment, and he looked away from those all-too-seeing eyes.

'We needed help with childcare,' he said, being distinctly frugal with the truth. 'We lost the live-in nanny, and Mum stepped up. That's why I took this job—to be closer to her.'

The red phone rang just as Emily opened her mouth, rescuing him from a conversation that was about to get into very tricky waters, and he sighed with relief as she scooped up the phone. The last thing he needed while he was at work was an in-depth discussion of his second failed marriage...

'Right, we've got a thirty-four-year-old woman, fall from a horse, query spinal injuries, short loss of consciousness, ETA ten minutes.'

She got away just about on time, and Elizabeth was there with the dog. There was no sign of Billy, of course, but Phoebe ran up to her, and she bent and hugged her as Billy and Amelie appeared.

Billy was chasing Oscar again around the playground, but Amelie ran over to her grandmother, her pink dungarees reassuringly grubby, with grass stains on the knees and bottom, and a blob of something that could have been tomato sauce on her unicorn T-shirt. She was beaming, and her smile reminded Emily so much of Oliver that her heart squeezed.

'Amelie, this is Emily,' Elizabeth said, and

Emily smiled at the child that could so easily have been hers.

'Hello, Amelie,' she said gently. 'It's nice to meet you. Billy told me you'd started in his class. This is Phoebe, by the way. Have you met?'

'I saw her at lunch,' Amelie said. 'Grandma, Lucy asked me on a play date. Can I go?'

'Not today, darling. We're going to Emily's house with Billy and Phoebe, but another day, I'm sure.'

Her face fell. 'Oh. OK. Can I go tomorrow?'

'Let me talk to Lucy's mummy tomorrow,' Elizabeth said, just as Billy ran up.

'Mummy, can we have pasta?'

Emily laughed and ruffled his hair. 'Again? We'll see. Amelie and her grandma are coming to ours now for a play date.'

'Cool,' he said, and then, 'can we have pizza instead?'

Elizabeth didn't really mention Oliver, but Emily did glean that Amelie's mother was based in Germany and made fleeting visits at the weekends.

'Gosh, doesn't Amelie miss her?' she asked, unable to imagine what it would be like to see Phoebe or Billy so little.

'Oh, yes, of course,' Elizabeth said, 'but I do what I can to fill in the gaps and we get by.'

She tilted her head and smiled at Emily. 'Enough of us. Tell me about yourself,' she said, switching the conversation back to Emily. 'I'm longing to hear all about you. I've often wondered what you were doing with your life, and Oliver tells me you're divorced. I'm sorry to hear that, but you seem to have made a lovely home for your children.'

'Thank you. I've done my best—'

And that was as far as any revelations went, because the children came running over, demanding pizza, and she ended up cooking for all three of them, and while they piled in, seeing who could eat the most pizza, the conversation moved to what she thought of the hospital.

'Oliver seems quite impressed,' she said, and Emily smiled wryly.

'Yes, I think he imagined it would be a bit quiet, but so far it's been pretty hectic. He's good, though. He's going to be an asset.'

'I'm glad. He was worried it would be the end of his career, I think, but Kath didn't really leave him any choice. The job in Germany was too good to turn down, and I couldn't really live in London with them long-term. My life's here now.'

'Yes, I was going to ask you about that,' she said, her curiosity getting the better of her. 'The last thing I knew you were living in Hampshire.'

'We were, but I moved up here when Martin died.'

That shocked her, and she reached out and laid a hand on Elizabeth's arm. 'Oh, no, I'm so sorry. When did he die?'

'Five and a half years ago. It was very sudden.'

'Oh, Elizabeth, I'm so sorry. You must have been absolutely devastated.'

'I was. I am.' She glanced away, staring at something in the distance. 'He had a heart attack out of the blue. I found him in the garden, on the bench under the trees. It must have been very, very quick. He looked so peaceful.'

'But what a shock for you.'

'It was. There was nothing wrong with him. He was fit and well and hadn't had so much as a twinge that I knew of. I keep telling myself it was better than a slow, lingering death or a horrible stroke that left him unable to move or communicate, but it doesn't stop me missing him every single day, and it'll always hurt that I never got to say goodbye. Anyway, I was rattling around in the house on my own, so I sold it and moved up here to be closer to my sister, and then Oliver needed my help with Amelie so—Amelie, no, don't fight over the last slice. That's rude, darling.'

'But he's had more than me!' she protested, and Billy denied it, but couldn't look her in the eye, so Emily solved the problem by giving it to Phoebe because she'd been left trailing by their competition.

'Sorry, he's a bit feral,' she said to Elizabeth, but she was laughing.

'Don't apologize. It's nice to see children with healthy appetites,' she said with a smile, then glanced at her watch. 'We ought to be going soon, but it's been lovely, Emily. It's so good to see you again. You must come to us next time. We only live round the corner.'

'That would be really nice,' she said, slightly torn because she wasn't sure if Oliver would be open to that. He'd looked a bit cagey earlier today, as if he hadn't wanted them together.

Why? She had no idea, and Elizabeth had been disappointingly discreet. She could always ask him about himself, but she wasn't sure she wanted to know about his complicated domestic arrangements, and she certainly didn't want to talk about her own messy life.

Which didn't stop her being curious…

* * *

Thankfully, James decided that Oliver's hand didn't need holding any more—not that it ever had, she was sure—so she was freed from the constant contact, the weird tug of tension in her chest every time he was in the room, which meant she could truly concentrate on her work.

And there was plenty of it. They were as busy as ever, so the days flew by, and before she knew it, it was the weekend.

She picked the children up from school on Friday, took them home and packed their things, and at five on the dot Steve appeared to take them to his.

'Be good,' she said automatically, but they'd gone, telling their father all about what they'd done this week, and she waved them off as they drove away, then closed the front door.

Silence.

Silence and emptiness, and she spared a thought for Elizabeth. How had she coped when Martin died? When she'd walked back in from the garden and knew the house was empty for ever?

Not that this was the same thing at all. Divorce was hardly in the same league as bereavement, but it still left its wounds.

She gave herself a mental shake, tackled the laundry, changed the sheets, put on another load and ran a bath. She was going to read a book, but she was already in the water by the time she realized she'd forgotten to bring it.

Which left her mind time to wander, which of course it did, without asking her permission, straight into Oliver territory.

What kind of a marriage did he have? It couldn't be much of one if Kath was in Germany all the time, but maybe that suited him? Suited both of them, perhaps, but Kath must be made of sterner stuff than her.

When Steve had moved back here to be with his first wife, Amanda, and their two children, it had left Emily, Billy and Phoebe bereft. He'd given up his whole new life and gone back to his old home, and she'd been left with no choice but to follow him here for the sake of her children, so they could maintain their relationship with him.

She knew why he'd done it, because like her he'd never got over his first love, so she could understand, even sympathize, but he'd destroyed her trust and left her sad and lonely.

Just as she'd been when Oliver had left her.

How different would their lives have been if she'd gone with him to Chicago? He'd wanted her to, he'd begged her to go, but her father was waiting for bypass surgery, and the prospect of being so far away if anything had happened to him had held her back. She'd told herself if she'd really meant that much to Oliver, he would have stayed, but in her heart she knew he couldn't. He'd signed up to a course, he'd paid for it, he was committed, and so he'd gone, and she'd kissed him goodbye and waited for him to come back.

Only he didn't, or not to her, because he'd met Sue and that had changed everything.

If only she'd gone, or he'd stayed, their lives would have been completely different. They might have had children of their own, but instead between them they'd had two failed marriages and four children, none of which would probably have existed if they'd stayed together.

But they hadn't, and painful though her break-up first with Oliver and then with Steve had been, she couldn't unwish her children, never in a million years, and she didn't imagine Oliver could unwish his, either.

But that didn't stop her wondering where they would have ended up if she'd gone, and what kind of a family they might have had—

Oh, for goodness' sake! She had to stop obsessing about him. Their relationship was over, done with long, long ago. Her fault? His? Whatever—it was over.

Except now he was here all the time, getting

inside her head, haunting her sleep and driving her crazy. Still, it was the weekend and James was on tomorrow, so she'd get a bit of respite...

CHAPTER THREE

SO MUCH FOR RESPITE. She walked into the department at seven the next morning and practically fell over him.

'What are you doing here? I thought James was on today. You've been here all week!' she said, and he shrugged and gave her a wry smile.

'I swapped. Connie's out and their childcare fell through, so I told James I'd cover the morning. Do you have a problem with that?'

She felt herself colour slightly. 'No—no, of course not. Sorry. I was just surprised.'

'Yeah, I got that. So how come you're here? You've been here all week, too.'

'It's Steve's weekend for the children, so I work both days.'

He cocked his head on one side and studied her thoughtfully. 'Do you do twelve days straight, or do you have time off next week?'

'No, I work twelve days, but ten of them

aren't full days. It's not ideal, but it's not as bad as it sounds and at least I pull my weight.'

'It still makes getting life stuff done tricky.'

She laughed at that. 'Isn't it always?' she said. Then she added, 'It's weirdly quiet without the kids, though, so I'd rather be at work. It feels odd and empty. They drive me mad, but when they aren't there, it feels all wrong. I mean, there's quiet, and there's too quiet.' Quiet enough to start thinking about him...

He nodded again, his mouth kicking up in a smile full of irony. 'Yeah. I know how that goes.' And then out of the blue he added, 'So what will you do this evening?'

'Oh, I have no idea. Put away the washing, I expect. It's the highlight of my weekend.'

He laughed, then pulled a thoughtful face. 'How do you fancy going to a pub? Nothing flashy, just a drink and something to eat?'

She stared at him, slightly stunned. 'Are you asking me on a date?'

'No!' he said hastily, and then softened it with a smile. 'No, not at all. I was asking if you want to come and hang out with an old friend so I can pretend to have a life that doesn't involve Amelie or work. I don't know anyone here, and it's a bit...'

'Lonely?' she offered, torn between contemplating the 'old friend' thing and wondering if things were all right with his rather odd marriage, and he nodded.

'Yeah, pretty much.' He gave a soft huff of laughter. 'Although it's hard to be lonely when I'm always surrounded by people, but...'

'Yes.'

'Yes?'

'Yes, it's hard, but it happens, and yes, that would be nice. Saturday night is always a bit dull somehow. Seven thirty?'

His mouth kicked up at one side. 'Sure. Amelie should be in bed by then. I'll check with my mother that she's OK to babysit, but I'm sure she will be and we won't be out late. Any idea where we could go?'

'Not really. I don't go out a lot, but James is a fan of the Harbour Inn down by the river mouth. We could try that?'

'OK. I'll check it out. In fact give me your phone. I'll put my number in and you can send me your address and I'll pick you up.'

She handed it over, wondering at the wisdom of agreeing to all this, and he tapped in his number and handed it back.

'Right, I suppose we ought to go and tackle the backlog from last night,' he said. 'I think they're still wading through the revellers. I don't know where the young get their stamina.'

'You mean you can't remember the nights

we stayed out till five and fell into bed for two hours before lectures?' she teased, and just like that she'd scrolled them back almost twenty years, the memories so vivid it could have been yesterday.

Her breath caught as he held her eyes, and then he turned away before she had a chance to read them properly.

'That was a very long time ago,' he said quietly, and headed off towards the desk, leaving her wondering why on earth she'd said that. So awkward. And they were going out tonight? So much for 'old friends'.

'Idiot,' she muttered, and followed him.

Why did she have to talk about bed?
And specifically their bed. He closed his eyes, breathed in and counted to ten, then picked up a file and headed towards the cubicles. Frustration was burning a hole in him, and he was annoyed with himself for reacting to her. Especially as they were now going on a 'not-a-date' date!

So much for taking her out for a nice platonic little chat...

What to wear?
It's not a date!
She rifled through her wardrobe, discount-

ing everything on the grounds of being too boring, too provocative, too bright, too tight, too loose—all her clothes were too something, and she sat down on the bed and sighed.

Jeans and a pretty top? Less controversial than a dress, and it wasn't really warm enough for sandals yet, not in the evening.

Jeans, then. Definitely jeans. And a totally uncontroversial top. She pulled them on, looked at herself and sighed. She looked as if she was going to the supermarket!

'Why did I say yes?' she wailed, and ripped the top off, going back to the wardrobe for an alternative. Better. Prettier, but still not overly dressy.

She checked the time, studied her face and decided it would do. Enough make-up to have made an effort, not so much that she looked as if she was going 'out' out.

A car pulled up outside, and she grabbed a cardi, slid her feet into simple ballet pumps and ran downstairs. She could see him through the obscured glass, a fuzzy shape heading to the front door, and she pulled it open as he reached for the bell.

How could he look so hot in jeans and a shirt?

He gave her a guarded smile. 'Hi. All ready?'

'Yup.' She scooped up her bag, locked the

front door and followed him back to the car, relieved that he was wearing the same sort of thing as her, less relieved at her reaction to it, which was doing nothing for her plan to keep it strictly neutral. She got in as he slid behind the wheel and glanced across at her.

'I've booked a table at the Harbour Inn—it seems to have good reviews, so I hope it's OK.'

'So do I, as I suggested it, but really I have no idea. My work–life balance means I'm either at work being a doctor, or at home being a mother, which is my life. I can't even remember the last time I was just me.'

He gave a soft laugh. 'You and me both, but we're doing it now, so let's go. You never know—we might even have fun.'

They pulled up in the car park, and over the top of the seawall she could see the masts of the dinghies on the foreshore silhouetted against the sky.

They went in and were ushered to a table by the window, and she looked around as they sat down. 'Oh, this is lovely.'

'Your choice,' he said with a smile, and she smiled back.

'Not really. I was going from what James said, but he clearly doesn't lie.'

They ordered drinks, pored over the menu

for a while and ended up with traditional fish and chips.

'Not the healthiest, but hey,' he said wryly. 'We can't be good all the time.'

'I try, but if I listened to Billy, we'd have pasta every night.'

That made him laugh. 'I don't have that problem. I hand over the money and all the responsibility for that to my mother and let her deal with it.'

'You're lucky to have her.'

His smile faded. 'Yes, I am, and I'm glad I'm there for her now Dad's not around, but I use her more than enough as it is, which is another reason why I hardly ever go out. I don't want to take advantage. It simply isn't fair.'

'Life isn't,' she said softly, then added, 'I was so sorry to hear about your father. He was such a lovely man. It must have been a terrible shock for all of you.'

He dropped his eyes. 'Yeah, it was awful. Very sudden. And it was right before Amelie was born as well, and I was gutted that he never got to meet her. And then Kath only took three months' maternity leave and went back to work as soon as we could get a live-in nanny, so I barely saw Mum in that time.'

'That must have been hard.'

'It was, juggling trying to keep an eye on

her and help her, find any time to bond with Amelie, not let my work colleagues down—it was a nightmare, but she was brilliant. They'd already talked about downsizing, so she sold the family home, bought herself a lovely flat in Woodbridge so she was closer to her sister, and then when the nanny left eighteen months ago, she dropped everything and stepped up without hesitating, and she's been amazing ever since. Then this job came up and I sold my house, she let the flat, and we've bought a house together.'

They all lived together? 'Gosh. And I thought my life was complicated! So how does Kath fit into all this?' she asked tentatively, and his mouth twisted into a rueful little smile.

'Ah. Yeah. Kath and I aren't together any more,' he told her, and her heart gave a little jolt. 'She's always travelled a lot with her job, but about a year ago she was offered a stunning promotion and she's now based in Germany, and there's a new man in her life, and we've both moved on.'

'And Amelie?'

'Lives with me full time. That was the deal in our divorce settlement. I wasn't losing another child to a broken marriage, and to be honest she wasn't the most involved of parents. I mean, don't get me wrong, she loves Amelie, and Amelie loves her, and she comes over from Germany whenever she can, but she simply doesn't have the time to devote to Amelie, and my mother does.'

'And are you happy?' she asked.

'In a way,' he said after a lengthy pause, and his eyes searched hers. 'What about you? You've been through a lot. Are *you* happy?'

She rolled her eyes. 'Gosh, that's a hard one. I would rather it had been different, but it is what it is, and yes, I'm happy, I suppose. I love my job, I love our little house and I adore my children, so I have a lot to be thankful for, but I'm never going there again. Divorce leaves its scars.'

'Yes, it does. It certainly does, but Kath and I—well, it was a disaster once Amelie was born, and to be fair it wasn't great before that. She basically wanted a house husband, someone happy to hold the fort and be there as and when she had time to come home to change the contents of her suitcase, and that was never going to be me. She understood my commitment to my job, because she had the same commitment to hers, but she had no commitment to our marriage, and that—'

He broke off, then said, 'I was going to say it hurt, but actually it just annoyed me more than anything, but I guess it was my fault.'

'How was it your fault?'

He shrugged. 'I should have realized what she was like, but I was grateful initially that she understood my work schedule. Or I thought she did, till the crunch came and she said I should give up my job. That was never going to happen, not at that stage in my training.'

'Could you both have cut back?'

His laugh was humourless and a little surprised. 'No way. It would have been career suicide for me, and she wouldn't even consider it, so we got a nanny and we managed, but it was never really satisfactory, not till Mum stepped up. Then all I felt was relief. As I said, it wasn't much of a marriage and it was definitely a mistake.'

'So how did you feel about Sue when you split up?'

His mouth tilted into a wry smile. 'Ah, well, that was a whole different ball game. We'd been back in the UK awhile, and she'd had Charlie, and I was working ridiculous hours—you know how that goes—and then she found a babysitter and enrolled on a cookery course one evening a week, and met a woman there called Donna. They had a lot in common—they were both from the States, they loved crafts, they loved cooking—and it dawned on them that they loved each other. Game over.'

'Wow,' she said softly. 'I wasn't expecting that.'

He laughed. 'No, nor was I, but let's just say it explained a lot of what was wrong with our marriage. I'd blamed it on my work schedule, but it wasn't that—or not all that, but it was what it was. There was no way I was in competition with Donna and at least it left my ego intact. Charlie was more of a worry, and I was gutted for him at first that we weren't going to be bringing him up together, but you know, Donna's lovely, Sue's happy with her, they're married, I'm still in regular contact with Charlie and he's happy, well-adjusted…'

His little shrug spoke volumes.

'But you're really not,' she said, realizing she could still read his eyes.

This time he didn't look away, and she could see the sadness in them as clear as day. 'No. No, I'm really not. Not with that. Not because of our marriage, that wasn't working anyway, and we really only got married because she was pregnant and it made it easier for residency and stuff, but Charlie… Now they're back in the States, I hardly see him in the flesh, and there's only so much you can gain from a video call, and I miss his hugs.'

She was sure he did. It must be heart-breaking. 'Did they *have* to go back?'

'Yes, they did. Donna's parents were ill, and she needed to be near them so there really wasn't an option, but—yeah, it hurts.'

'And you couldn't go back because of Amelie. Oh, Oliver, that must have been so hard. I can't imagine how I'd feel if that was Billy.'

He shook his head. 'No. You can't, not till it happens. You think you understand, but—I had no idea. He was so much a part of my life. I saw him whenever I could, and losing him like that was really tough. And there was no way we could move there, so I stayed here with Amelie while Kath invested all her energy into her career and I tried to hold mine together and maintain my relationship with Charlie, and this is how it's all ended up.' He laughed again, but his eyes were still sad. 'Great, isn't it? I'm forty-two, divorced twice, and I'm back living with my mother. Happy days.'

'It's not quite like that,' she said gently, but he just gave a little huff of what could have been laughter but sounded more like self-mockery.

'No. No, it's not quite like that, but it feels like it. So anyway, that's me. I want to know about you.' He cocked his head on one side. 'Mum said the children had fun the other day.'

'They had a fight over the last slice of pizza,' she pointed out, and he laughed.

'Yes, she said. She also said they were lovely together.'

She chuckled. 'They were, in between times.'

His smile faded. 'So what went wrong with you and Steve?' he asked softly. 'How did you end up here?'

She wasn't sure she wanted to talk about it, but he'd spilled his guts, so it was only fair. But...

'Well?' he said, just as their meals arrived, and she picked up her knife and fork.

She hesitated, wondering where to start with the sorry saga of her failed marriage. 'I don't know where to start.'

'The beginning?' he said, his smile gentle.

She smiled, picked up a chip as a stalling tactic, put it down in defeat and did as he suggested.

'OK. I was working in Nottingham, I met Steve, and I knew all about his ex and his two boys—he was quite upfront about the fact he saw them every other weekend, and I was pleased he felt the need to keep in touch, so I was fine with it and we seemed happy enough. Anyway, we got married and had the children, and Steve was back there every other weekend and for a week at a time in school holidays, staying in his old house with his ex and the kids, and then it slowly dawned on them that they still loved each other, always had done, and they wanted to be together.'

He frowned. 'Ouch.'

'Absolutely. It came totally out of the blue, but they were quite certain, they'd thought about it for a long time, so we split up and he moved back to them, and every other weekend he was coming up to me.'

'And?' he prompted as she hesitated.

'And it felt wrong. I didn't like him being in my space, the children were confused about Daddy not being there all the time, they didn't understand why we were in different bedrooms, and in the holidays he took them to his other house and they'd come back after a week really confused and unhappy. It just wasn't working, not for any of us. He was really unhappy about leaving the little ones, but it was right for him and his other family.'

'They couldn't have moved to Nottingham?'

She shook her head. 'No, his kids are in secondary school and one of them has a learning disability, so it really wasn't an option to unsettle them.'

'Ah. That's tough.'

'It was tough, tough on all of us, but it was the right thing for them. I was still in my old job for a little while, but then Laura's maternity leave post came up and it had my name written all over it, because Steve's only ten miles away. There were actually two posts going, so I said I'd do eight tenths, but short days and working every other weekend, with more time off in the holidays, and that gives me time with the children, but it's not really ideal and James would love me to do more. That's why I do the weekends when I can to make up for it, but it seems to be working a lot better for all of us.'

He studied her thoughtfully. 'You're very understanding.'

'What, like you with Sue and Donna? Sometimes you just have to deal with what life throws at you and move on, so I did. And anyway, when I look back on it, our marriage was far from perfect, and I wouldn't have stood in his way even if I could. This way we're all better off.'

He chuckled and shook his head. 'What a pair we are. Four kids, three marriages, two compromised careers—'

'Stop,' she said firmly. 'Stop right there. You have your mother, you have two children who you love and who love you, you have a good job in an excellent hospital, even if it's not the cushy little number you thought it was going to be—'

'I never said anything about wanting a cushy little number!'

'Well, that's good, because you aren't going to get it in Yoxburgh. And I've got two beautiful, healthy children who I adore, a job I love, a house I can just about afford—what more could either of us want? We have so much to be thankful for.'

He studied her face, a slow smile tilting his lips, and he stifled a grin at the last second. 'I'd forgotten how gorgeous you are when you get feisty,' he murmured, 'and you need to eat that if you're going to or it'll be stone-cold,' he added softly, and went back to his own food, that smile still playing around the corners of his mouth.

She picked up her cutlery again and picked at the remains of her fish, but his words were echoing in her head.

'I'd forgotten how gorgeous you are when you get feisty...'

There was a touch of colour in her cheeks, and he was busy kicking himself for saying what he had, but hell, she was glorious when she got on her high horse. He'd forgotten that—forgotten all sorts of things, like how easy she was to talk to, how honest she was about her feelings, how responsive she'd been...

He cut his thoughts off sharp, and leaned back in the chair.

'I'm stuffed.'

She put her knife and fork down and met his eyes, then looked away. 'Yes, me, too. I don't think I can finish this. It's a killer.'

'Probably in more ways than one, but it was delicious.'

'It was. Pity, the dessert menu looked really wicked.'

'We could share?'

Their eyes met and held, and she looked away first. 'Depends. What did you fancy?'

You...

'The chocolate fondant?' he suggested, knowing it was her favourite. 'I love a melting middle chocolate pudding.'

'Cream or ice cream?'

'Ooh. I'll let you choose,' he said, knowing she'd say cream. And...

'Cream.'

Right on cue. He smiled. 'Done.'

Except sharing was tricky. Too intimate, too cosy, too reminiscent...

He found himself watching her every spoonful, and he was relieved when it was over and she stopped sighing with delight over every bite.

'Oh, that was good,' she said, and he wiped his mouth and nodded.

'It was. Good choice. Coffee?'

'No, thanks. I think I'm done, but don't let me stop you.'

He met her eyes, and for once he couldn't read them.

'OK. I'll get the bill.'

He drove her home, pulled up outside and looked across at her.

'Thank you for coming out. It was really good to do something normal.'

'Yes, it was. Thank you for taking me.' And then before her brain could take over from her tongue, she added, 'I could make you a coffee? I know you wanted one.'

He hesitated and she could see him looking at her, but it was too dark to read his eyes. And then he spoke, his voice a little odd somehow. 'Yeah, why not? That would be nice.'

They went in, and she flicked on the lights and led him through to the kitchen, thankful that she'd had a blitz the night before, and he looked around.

'This is lovely. I like what you've done with it.'

'I haven't really done very much, and to be honest it wasn't difficult because it's so small, but it does the job and I couldn't afford anything more.'

'Do you need anything more?'

She smiled. 'Not really. A playroom would be nice, or another room downstairs, but that would mean moving or extending and I can't afford to do either. We're warm, we're dry, we're fed and we're happy. What more could we need?'

He shook his head slowly, and his smile was gentle. 'You always were good at putting a positive spin on things,' he murmured, and she laughed.

'Was I? Or was it just a case of learning it out of necessity? Anyway, tea or coffee?'

He hesitated, mostly because, standing in the small kitchen with her, he could smell the enticing fragrance that had teased his senses all evening and stirred up a hornet's nest of want and need and frustration. Not to mention longing.

Get a grip, man. You aren't going there again.

She turned round, two mugs in her hand, and raised an eyebrow. 'Hello?'

'Sorry, I was miles away. What did you say?'

She sighed and smiled. 'Tea or coffee? I have decaf, if you want?'

No, it's you I want...

'Decaf coffee would be lovely. Thanks.'

'You go and sit down, then. I'll bring it through,' she said, and turned back to the mugs, so he retreated to the living room, wondering why he'd agreed to come in, but he was here now, so he took the few moments he had to look around.

She was right, it was small, but it worked, with a dining table at the garden end beside the kitchen, and a big comfy looking sofa under the window at the other end.

One end of the sofa had a table with an open book lying face down on it, so he headed for the other end and sat down, hopefully far enough away that he wouldn't be able to smell her.

Except she brought the coffee over and put it down next to him, and left a subtle drift of scent behind that did nothing at all to settle down his raging libido. Nor did the way she curled up on the sofa, tucking her now bare feet under her bottom and wrapping her hands around her mug.

'It's been really nice spending time with you again,' he said softly, and she turned her head and met his eyes.

'Yes. It's been a very long time.'

'It has. A lot of water under all sorts of bridges.'

'Most of them leading to divorce,' she added wryly. 'And the odd lucky escape.'

'Really?' That shocked him a little, although why he wasn't sure.

Her smile was wry and a little bitter. 'Yeah, really. I nearly married another doctor, but we were like ships in the night. We shared the same bed, but hardly ever together, and it was like having a flat-mate. And then he got a different job, so did I, so we just split up and went our separate ways.'

'Like me and Kath.'

'Yes, except we didn't have any children, so there was no guilt, just disillusionment, really, and disappointment. So I picked myself up and vowed never again, and then a few years later I met Steve, and he worked from home and was flexible so we could actually have a life together. I thought it would be fine, only I was wrong and it all fell apart. And of course, this time there were children involved—two sets.'

'I'm sorry. Life stinks sometimes.'

'Yes, it does.' And then she added, totally out of the blue, 'I often wonder if it would have been any better if I'd gone with you to Chicago.'

Her voice was a little wistful, and for some

reason it made his heart beat faster. 'Why didn't you?' he asked quietly, and she gave him a sad little smile.

'You know why. My father was ill. I couldn't. And anyway, we hadn't been together that long, I'd already accepted a placement starting that summer and I had debts. I needed to get on with my career, start to earn some money, and there was no guarantee I could find a job over there, you were going to be busy on your postgrad course—'

'You could have enrolled for the course.'

'But I didn't want to. I couldn't afford it, and anyway, my father was waiting for a heart bypass and I was worried I'd be hours away if anything happened. But I did regret it, for a long time.'

He let that sink in, then searched her eyes and asked the question that had nagged at him for years.

'Did you love me?'

Her mouth opened, and she closed it and looked away, then looked back, her eyes sad.

'Yes. Yes, I loved you—but I wasn't enough for you, was I? You found Sue and that was that. I thought you'd be back after a year—I was waiting for you—but you weren't, or at least not on your own, so I moved on with my life, but I missed you.'

He swallowed. 'I missed you, too.'

'So why did you sleep with Sue?'

He couldn't hold her eyes, couldn't bear the rawness in her steady gaze, so he looked away.

'I have no idea. I'd seen her around at the college, and I went to a party and she was there, and we ended up together. She was warm and sweet and funny, and I guess we'd both had a bit too much to drink, and we just ended up in bed. And then a few weeks later she told me she was pregnant and I was devastated, but she was young and innocent, and I didn't feel I had a choice except to stand by her, even if it meant the end for you and me. And yes, it was a mistake, no, I shouldn't have done it, but it gave me Charlie, and I love him more than I knew it was possible to love anyone. He's such a huge part of my life I couldn't imagine what it would be like without him, so I couldn't turn the clock back. No Charlie, no Amelie...'

She nodded slowly, her face sad. 'No. I couldn't turn it back, either. Billy and Phoebe are everything to me, and they have to come first, before anything, but if it helps, I did love you, and not going with you broke my heart.'

'I'm sorry,' he said, his voice gruff, and he

looked away, blinking back sudden uninvited tears.

'Don't be,' she said softly. 'We both did what we had to do. The decisions had already been made, and we were both committed.'

He met her eyes again. 'I didn't need to sleep with Sue,' he pointed out bluntly, and her smile tore his heart.

'No, you didn't, but you didn't abandon her, either. I couldn't have forgiven you for that. And as you said before, there's a lot of water gone under a lot of bridges. We've both made mistakes. We're human. We have to learn from them and move on.'

Learn from them? So what the hell was he doing here now?

He put his mug down and stood up. 'I need to go,' he said, his voice a little gruff to his ears, and she uncoiled her legs and stood up and walked with him to the door.

He stopped in front of it, stared down into her eyes, and with a resigned sigh he pulled her gently into his arms and hugged her, burying his face in her hair and breathing her in for an age before he dropped his arms.

She eased away and looked up at him, her lips just a breath away from his, damp and slightly parted.

Don't do it...

With a ragged sigh he took a step back, and with a quiet, 'Goodnight, Emily,' he turned and opened the door and walked out of her house.

She watched him stride away, get into the car and drive off, lifting a hand in farewell, and she closed the door, leant on it and touched a hand to her lips.

Had she imagined it, or had he nearly kissed her? She could still feel the touch of his breath on her skin, the shiver of anticipation, the yearning need—or had she just imagined it?

Of course she had. And even if he hadn't nearly kissed her, it was too late for them now. It had been too late for close on twenty years.

She scooped up the mugs, put them in the dishwasher and went upstairs to bed.

At least she'd get some respite tomorrow. A whole day without him.

Suddenly it didn't seem all that appealing...

CHAPTER FOUR

'HELLO, DARLING. I didn't expect you back so early. Did you have a lovely time?'

'Yes, thanks. It was very nice.' Right up until the time he hugged her...

He bent and kissed his mother's cheek, and dropped onto the sofa beside her. 'How about you? Was Amelie good for you, or has she been up?'

'She was up for a little while, but not long. She just wanted some time with her Grandma.'

'I bet you spoiled her.'

'We might have read a book or two.'

'Or three,' he said, smiling indulgently at her. 'Honestly, you're a star, Mum, but you are such a pushover.'

'And you never spoil her, of course.' She chuckled and got stiffly to her feet. 'I'm off to bed. I'll see you tomorrow.'

'Anything I can do?'

'No, no, everything's done. Just relax. You don't do that nearly often enough. Sleep well.'

'You, too. And thanks again.'

'You're welcome. I'm glad you enjoyed it.'

She kissed his cheek, gave it a little pat and walked through into her part of the house, her book tucked under her arm, and he watched her go, torn between gratitude and guilt.

Well, it made a change from frustration, he thought as he went upstairs to check on Amelie. She was fine, sleeping peacefully, and he bent and kissed her tousled hair, then came down and sat on the sofa, scrolling through messages on his phone.

One from Charlie, saying there was something he wanted to tell him. He glanced at the time. It would be mid-afternoon in Boston.

The phone rang once, and Charlie picked up, the sound of his voice instantly grounding, and his whole life fell back into place. This was who he was, the father of two wonderful children, not some crazy hormonal undergraduate.

He settled back and listened to his son.

Work the next day was as busy as ever, with loads of sporting injuries as a result of the lovely weather.

Luckily most of it was routine stuff, because she was struggling to concentrate.

Had he been going to kiss her? She had no idea, but for a breathless second she'd wondered, and she'd dreamt about him last night...

She made herself concentrate, and by the end of her shift she was exhausted, her brain was reeling and her feet were numb, but the second she walked in through her front door, she was straight back to that not-quite kiss.

Madness. It would be folly to start something like that with him.

Wouldn't it?

What if—no. Bad idea.

She heard the scrunch of tires as Steve's car pulled up on the drive, putting a stop to her endless circular thoughts.

'See you in two weeks,' their father said, kissing the children goodbye, and they shut the door and ran in and hugged her, fizzing with excitement.

'They've got a puppy, Mummy,' Phoebe said, eyes sparkling, and her heart sank.

'That's nice,' she said, waiting for the inevitable. She didn't have to wait long.

'Mummy, please, *pleeeeease* can we have a puppy, too?' Phoebe said, her eyes wide with longing.

She gave a tiny sigh. 'You know we can't, darling. My work schedule won't allow it.'

'But Amelie's got a dog and her daddy's a doctor, too, so you could,' Billy reasoned.

'But her grandma lives with them, and it's her dog,' she said, crossing her fingers behind her back and hoping she wasn't lying.

'So why can't *our* grandma live with us?' he asked, and she sighed again.

'Because she and Grandad live near Nottingham, Billy. You know that.'

'But they could move,' he said with all the logic of childhood. 'We moved to be near Daddy.'

And left her parents behind... She swallowed a little ache. 'I know. I'd like them closer, too, but they live where they live, and they've got lots of friends there, so they aren't going to move, and besides, we haven't got room for them here. Anyway, tell me all about this puppy. What's it called?'

He was back in the ED by seven Monday morning, leaving his mother to deal with a fractious Amelie who'd apparently decided she hated school.

He didn't have time to dwell on it, though, because he was straight into Resus, taking over from the team that had been working for the last hour on Dylan Reed, a teenager who'd fallen from a height.

'So what's the story?' he asked Sam, and was told he'd sneaked out of his bedroom window and was coming home drunk and/or drugged and had slipped and fallen backwards off the drainpipe onto the patio below.

'Pupils are equal and reactive, but a bit sluggish, and he's been semi-conscious throughout but he's not really making any sense. Reflexes are weak in the lower limbs and his right arm, so we're looking at head and spine. There's no obvious disruption on palpation but something's going on. He's booked for a CT shortly, and in the meantime we've done a tox screen and we're waiting on the results. Parents are in the family room and I'll go and talk to them now and update them. Over to you.'

'Great. Thanks. Anything else going on in the department I should know about?'

'Not as far as I'm aware. Have a good day.'

Oliver grunted and turned his attention to the boy. 'Right, is he good to go down to CT?' he asked, checking his stats on the monitor, and they nodded.

'Yes, he's stable.'

'OK. I'll go down with him and have a look,' he said, not liking the sound of the sluggish pupils or the weak reflexes. Drugs, or head and neck injuries—either way he was still far from ideal.

* * *

He was right to be worried, as it turned out. There was a small brain contusion, and what looked like bruising on the spinal cord, but there was nothing more to do in the ED, so he was shipped up to Paediatric HDU, pending the result of the drugs screen, and his parents went with him after an update, torn between worry over his condition and anger that he'd been so stupid.

He could empathize with that. It was how he felt about Charlie from time to time, but he had minimal control from so far away, which made it easier in that he didn't know when to worry about him, harder because it just meant there was a low-grade stress going on all the time.

Still, at least he was coming over for three weeks in June, so that was something to look forward to.

And then Emily walked in and gave him a slightly forced smile that didn't quite reach her eyes, and his stress levels ramped up again.

'Hi there. Good weekend?' she asked lightly.

He grimaced and looked away, cross with himself for whatever it was that had made their relationship strained. They'd been OK last week. Now? Not so much, apparently, probably after that almost-kiss moment. Or him spilling his guts. He ignored that and answered her question.

'Up and down. Charlie's decided to come over in June, for three weeks, which is the up. The down, Amelie's decided she hates school.'

'Really? She looked happy enough in the playground this morning. She ran off with Billy and Phoebe, and they were all giggling.'

He felt one layer of tension ease, replaced by another, the never-ending tug of war between his brain and his body. Or was it his heart?

'That's good to know.'

The silence yawned, and he was almost begging for the red phone to ring when she spoke.

'Are you OK?'

'Of course I am.'

'Are you? Are you really?'

Her voice was soft, teasing his senses, and he met her eyes and read concern behind the wariness.

He gave up the pretence. 'No. Not really,' he told her, going for honesty. 'Can we grab a coffee later?'

She hesitated a moment, then nodded.

'Sure. Of course. Assuming we get time.'

Big assumption. It was a quarter to two by the time they paused for breath, and they went straight to the Park Café, grabbed drinks and something to eat, and sat on a bench in the shade of a tree.

'So, what's wrong?' she asked, because something obviously was. 'Is it Charlie? Amelie?'

He shook his head slowly. 'No.'

No? Then...

'Is this about Saturday?' she asked, probing deeper.

He met her eyes, his still wary but steady on hers as he nodded. 'Maybe. We got into a lot of stuff, and...'

'And?' she coaxed as he trailed off, and he shrugged.

'I keep thinking we should have left it alone.'

'Why? It was good to know what you've been doing. We were together briefly half a lifetime ago, and I still care about you, but we're different people now, things have changed us, and it was really great to catch up and find out more about you now, about where you've been and what you've come through.'

He looked away. 'I just don't want it to change things, to make them awkward. I don't want you thinking—we can't go back, Emily. Even if we want to. There's too much at stake—the kids—all of it.'

She reached out and laid her hand over his. 'I don't want to go back. Believe me, I'm not looking to find another relationship to screw up. It would just be really nice to be friends.'

He looked back at her, his eyes doubtful, and then he gave a quiet sigh and his mouth tilted into a sad little smile.

'Yes. Yes, it would.' He looked away again. 'We are screwed up, aren't we? Both of us, in our own way.'

'I suppose we are. How does that song go? "Pick yourself up, dust yourself off and start all over again"? Except I can't even think about the last bit. I have bigger fish to fry now, and so do you, so that's OK. We understand each other. Friends?'

He reached out and cupped her cheek in a firm but gentle hand. 'Friends,' he said softly, and raised his coffee cup to her.

She clinked hers against it, as far as you could clink a paper cup, and smiled sadly.

'Good. And don't worry about Amelie. She'll be fine. They all go through this, and you've got Charlie's visit to look forward to.'

He nodded, bit into his sandwich and was about to take another bite when the pagers leaped into life.

'And here we go again.' He sighed, and they walked quickly back, eating as they went, binning the last bites as they went through the door, but her heart was lighter.

A friend was exactly what she needed in her life, especially one who was on the same page. No misunderstandings, no false expectations, no hidden agenda. Just friends...

He felt hugely relieved after their little chat, and working together was infinitely easier.

Amelie seemed to be settling in school, despite her protests, and his mother was making a few friends at the school gate, other grandmothers on childcare duty doing the school run.

She'd invited Emily and the children back to theirs for a play date, and he crossed his fingers it would go well and Amelie wouldn't have a strop about something trivial, but he didn't hold out much hope. She seemed to have a reluctance to let people close, having reeled them in in the first place.

Because of Kath's absence? Maybe. She was supposed to be coming over this weekend, but that always left Amelie tearful and fractious, and he wasn't sure he wanted her to come at all.

Except she didn't come. She deferred it, sending him a text on Thursday, while he was working with Emily.

'Oh, for heaven's sake! She can't keep doing this,' he growled, and Emily raised an eyebrow.

'Who can't do what?' she asked, and he dropped his phone back in his pocket and met her eyes.

'Kath. She was coming this weekend to see Amelie, but now she can't. Something more important has come up.'

His words were loaded with sarcasm, and Emily frowned.

'What's more important than not letting her daughter down?' she asked, and he swore.

'Exactly. It's ridiculous. Apparently someone's flying over from Japan, an important client, and she has "no choice".'

Emily hmphed and went back to writing up her notes, and he did a bit of hmphing himself, went and got a cold drink from the staff kitchen, and was tempted to throw it over his head to cool himself down.

And then the following weekend she couldn't manage Friday, and said she'd come on Saturday afternoon instead, and he was so angry he nearly told her not to bother.

He really, really didn't want to see her. Hard to avoid it, considering she was going to be in the house—unless she took Amelie somewhere else for the weekend? She might. Or he could take himself off somewhere and leave her to it. His mother was away for the weekend, staying with her sister, so maybe he could hide out in her part of the house.

Although Amelie would know he was there and would keep coming in, defeating the object.

He was slumped over the desk with his head in his hands when Emily walked into Resus.

He straightened up and swivelled round, and she eyed him thoughtfully. 'What's up?' she asked, and he shrugged.

'Kath. Again.'

'What again? Not the weekend?'

'Not the whole weekend, no, but she can't come tomorrow, she can't come till Saturday afternoon, so Amelie will be gutted, all over again, and to make it worse, because she was coming, Mum's going away, so it'll just be the three of us in the house and I'm so cross I could kill her.'

'You don't mean that.'

'No, of course I don't mean it literally, but it's just going to be difficult, and if I'm there they won't get the one-to-one.'

'You could always hide out at mine,' she said, and he searched her eyes, so wanting to say yes, but she was only being kind. Wasn't she?

'Really?'

'Really. The kids are with Steve, I'm at work,

and you can have Billy's room. It's got a decent bed in it, so you can even stay over if you want and leave them to it.'

She was actually serious. His heart thumped a little, and he ignored it, but it was so tempting...

'No, I can't do that,' he said after too long a hesitation, and she smiled.

'Well, you can, and you're very welcome to,' she said matter-of-factly, 'but you can cook for me if you like so I don't have to when I get home, if it makes you feel better.'

He was so, so tempted, but he shook his head slowly.

'No. It's not fair.'

'Why not?'

Because I still want you...

'Because it's the only downtime you get, the only time you can do stuff.'

'And it gets very dull. There's only a certain amount of fun you can have cleaning the house and doing the washing. If it makes you feel better, you can cut the grass and weed the garden while I'm at work.'

That made him chuckle, but he still shook his head.

'No. It's very kind of you, but no. I don't want to take advantage of you.'

'I don't think I asked you to,' she retorted

with a grin, 'but suit yourself. The offer's there. Take it or leave it.'

And with that she walked out and left him staring after her.

It's too dangerous.

He growled softly, closed the file, and got up and followed her out.

Would he come?

She wasn't sure, but to be on the safe side she changed the sheets and cleaned the house on Friday night after the children had gone, and she sent him a text when she got to work on Saturday morning.

Key under blue plant pot on right, mower in the garden shed, key in kitchen by door. Feel free. X

She pressed send, then instantly regretted the kiss. Too late. He'd make of it what he would and she had bigger things to think about because the revellers had been out in force. Three stabbings overnight, one still in Resus with his chest open when she hurried in there to help.

Tom was there, up to his wrists in the young man's lungs, trying to stem the bleed without any success.

'We're waiting on a surgeon,' he said, 'but I didn't think we had time to do that and it turns out I was right. Emily, could you do me a favour and get through to cardiothoracics and NAG. I need advice on this if we aren't going to lose him. Oh, hang on, I've got the bleeder. Clamp, please.'

The door swished open, and a CT consultant came in, took one look at him and shrugged. 'Well, you seem to be doing my job OK,' he said, and she heard Tom chuckle in relief.

'Pure luck. He's all yours,' he said, and stood back and let the CT consultant take over.

'What on earth was going on last night?' Emily asked as they wheeled the man away to Theatre. 'It sounds like carnage.'

'It was. It all kicked off at two this morning, apparently. They were all drunk, there were drugs involved, two gangs of youths—just utter carnage. We lost one, stabilized one and shipped him out, and this lad didn't seem too bad, and then he just suddenly went downhill. They're just kids. It's sickening what they're doing to each other. Anyway, I'm done, I think the worst is over and I'm going home now. Enjoy.'

Not a chance.

As the last of the overnight admissions were being dealt with, the usual 'we've got the weekend off so let's tackle the DIY/garden/ guttering' brigade turned up, together with a succession of sporting injuries—a dislocated shoulder, a squash ball in the eye, a dislocated kneecap—which kept her busy for the rest of her shift.

By the time she clocked off, she was tired, hungry, mildly irritated and more than ready to crawl into a hot bath and do nothing.

And then she turned onto her drive and found Oliver's car there, and her heart skipped a beat.

'Hello?' she said, walking in and kicking off her shoes, and he came out of the kitchen, bringing a waft of something delicious with him.

'You're here,' she said, unnecessarily, and he smiled.

'Yeah, sorry, I took you up on your offer, but I've mowed the lawn, weeded the beds, swept the patio and cooked you supper.'

She laughed. 'I can tell. You don't need to apologize—it smells amazing.'

'It's just chilli, but I wasn't sure what time you finished, so I did something that would keep hot for hours. How was your day?'

'Crazy. It started with stabbings, and ended up with the usual sporting injuries and peo- ple who have no idea of how to keep themselves safe when they do stuff they're clearly not qualified to do.'

'Oops. I'm guessing DIY?'

'And walking backwards with a rotary lawn-mower and falling down a slope with it on top of you. Luckily it had stalled before it did too much damage, but he had multiple severe cuts, he was soaked in petrol, and he'd landed on his hip on the path below and driven the head of his femur into his acetabulum, causing a lovely starburst fracture.'

'Ouch. I thought those mowers had an automatic cutout?'

'Not if they're ancient. And then there was the elderly woman who fell off a ladder and down the stairs trying to put stuff in the loft without help, and the guy who slashed his hand in half trying to lay a carpet—need I go on?'

He was laughing by then, and he shook his head. 'I get the drift. Do you want to change and shower, or just eat?'

'Do you know what I really want?'

'A hot bath and a nice cold glass of wine?' he asked, and she stifled a laugh.

'How did you guess?' she said, and he opened the fridge and poured her a glass of perfectly chilled Chardonnay.

'Enjoy,' he said, and she took it from him and went upstairs, her heart suddenly lighter.

* * *

He poured himself a glass, went into the living room and tried not to think about her lying naked in the bath somewhere above him.

He hadn't had to guess what she'd want. His mind scrolled back to the times he'd sat on the floor in the bathroom, chatting to her while she lay in the bath after a long day. Sometimes he'd share it with her, but always, always, when she was done, he'd wrap her in a towel and carry her to bed.

Don't go there. You'll just make it worse.

Hard to imagine how. Oh, this was such a mistake—although looking at her as she'd walked through the door, she hadn't looked like someone who was relishing cooking a meal before she could relax. He could understand that. The weekends were often killers, peppered with tragedy and liberally sprinkled with accidents that should never have happened.

He tipped his head back and rested it against the sofa, eyes closed, yet again trying not to think of her body lying naked just a few feet above him. It wasn't fair, and it wasn't why he was here. She'd offered him a way out of a difficult situation, and he'd taken her up on it and done some things to help her in return.

Because they were friends. Friends. Not lovers, not even contemplating it.

He heard the gurgle of water, and went back to the kitchen to reheat the chilli. She wouldn't be long, he guessed, and he sliced thick chunks off the fresh, squishy tiger bread and put them in a bowl, carried it through to the table, and stirred the chilli, just as she came running down the stairs.

'Oh, that smells so good—tiger bread? Oh, you are amazing!' she said, and before he knew what was happening, she slid her arms around him from behind and hugged him briefly, then let go and stood back.

'Anything I can do?'

'Ah—yeah, you could find the soured cream and the grated cheese in the fridge and take them through,' he said, his mind and body totally scrambled by the hug. 'I won't be a moment. You could use a mat on the table—this is hot.'

She left, and he sucked in a low, slow breath and blew it out even slower, then picked up the pot of chilli and followed her.

'That was so good,' she said, putting down her fork and leaning back against the chair, too tired to sit up straight any more. 'Thank you. I was starving.'

'You're welcome,' he said, and topped up her glass. 'Go and sit down and put your feet up, and I'll clear the table.'

'That's not fair,' she protested, but he just quirked an eyebrow at her and jerked his head towards the sofa, and she stifled a smile and went. If it made him feel better to wait on her, then she was fine with that.

She sat down, rested her head back and closed her eyes, and a short while later she heard his quiet tread, and felt the sofa dip as he sat down at the other end.

'Give me your feet,' he said, and she turned her head and looked at him. 'Come on. You know you want to.'

She gave up the inward battle she really didn't want to win, turned round on the sofa, put them up and closed her eyes as he set his thumbs to work, massaging the sole of her right foot.

'Oh, that's amazing,' she groaned as he finished. 'You always did give the best foot massage.'

'We aim to please. Other foot?'

How could feet be so sexy?

Except hers were, and always had been. Perfectly shaped, with neat, straight toes and a perfect arch. She'd always painted the nails way back when, but not now. Now they were bare, translucent, neatly clipped.

She'd rested her head back and closed her eyes, but she made the odd tiny sound as he worked, and when he stopped, she opened her eyes and smiled lazily.

'That was lovely. Thank you.'

'My pleasure. You look tired.'

She laughed, a soft little huff of sound filled with irony. 'I'm always tired. It's a constant juggling act, trying to balance my job with caring for the children and giving them the love and the opportunities they deserve.'

He nodded slowly. 'Yeah. I completely get that. If it wasn't for my mother, I'd be sunk. At least you have Steve reasonably close and he's doing his bit.'

'Oh, absolutely. I couldn't possibly work the hours I do if it wasn't for his input, and they all get on well now, so I don't need to worry about them when they're with him.'

He gave a soft huff of laughter. 'You're so lucky having him close. If only Kath could do more, but it is what it is.' He dredged up a smile. 'Can I get you another drink? Tea, coffee, fruit tea?'

She studied him thoughtfully, a little smile playing around her mouth. 'You're being very solicitous. Are you trying to earn brownie points?'

That made him laugh. 'No, I'm just being a decent human being. You've been at work all day. I haven't.'

'But you work longer hours and this is your time off.'

He lifted her feet off his lap and stood up. 'I really don't think making you a drink counts as work. I'm having decaf tea. You're having…?'

'Blackcurrant, please.'

He nodded and went into the kitchen, put the kettle on, found a container for the rest of the chilli and put it in the fridge, added the pan to the dishwasher and switched it on, then turned to find her propped in the door, watching him.

'You are super domesticated. What happened?'

'What happened? Um—I grew up?'

That made her chuckle, and the sound rippled through him like a tiny electric shock along his nerve endings.

He turned back to the kettle, and she came over to him, reaching past him to put the teabags back in the cupboard, and the scent from her skin was so enticing, so evocative that he groaned out loud.

'What?' she said, turning to look at him, and he put the kettle down with a sigh.

'I can't do this,' he said, his voice low and hushed. 'Deal with this—whatever it is, this tug, this undercurrent between us. It was always there, but that was fine then, and it's not fine now. It was half a lifetime ago, and we aren't those people any more. We've changed, and yes, I want you, but I don't know if the you I want is the old you, or who you are now, and it's getting in the way of everything,' he said, the confession dragged out of him. 'I'm not sure I even know who you are now, but I know I'm not who I was then, not by a mile.'

She held his eyes for a moment, hers soft and luminous, filled with sadness. 'Nor am I. I want you, too, but I can't trust myself, my own judgement, because maybe I just want to turn the clock back, and we can't do that. I never want another relationship where my children are exposed to hurt, and I'm sure you don't, either, so we can't let ourselves get sucked into anything that might affect them. And if it means our lives are a loveless desert, so be it, but I can't risk my kids' happiness, and nor can you. I just know we can't go back to what we had, because it's gone for ever. It died when you slept with Sue, and I don't know if I'll ever be able to trust you again.'

He turned away, his eyes prickling with sudden tears for all they'd lost, all he'd thrown away.

'I'm so sorry I hurt you,' he said, his voice broken, and he sucked in a breath and let it out again. 'I never meant...'

She slid her arms around him and rested her head against his back, and her warmth seeped into him.

'I know,' she said softly. 'We were too young, too foolish, too far apart, and if I'd been able to come with you, who knows how different it might have been, but it is what it is, and we're where we are now, and if we can somehow find a middle ground where we can be friends and still keep our hearts safe, then I'd love that. I need a friend right now far more than I need a lover, and I think you do, too. Someone we can talk to, someone who understands where we're coming from, someone we can understand. And that's so rare, so precious.'

He nodded slowly, and turned towards her, pulling her gently into his arms and holding her for the longest time. Her head was on his shoulder, his cheek against her hair, and he could feel the beat of her heart against his, the rise and fall of her chest as she breathed, the warmth of her body thawing the ache of loneliness deep inside him.

'I've missed you,' he said gruffly, and she sighed.

'I've missed you, too. It's good to have you back.'

She took a step back and looked up into his eyes, resting a hand against his cheek in a tender gesture that nearly broke him.

'I'm going to bed. I'll see you in the morning.'

He nodded and watched her go, his resolve in tatters, his heart aching.

I don't know if I'll ever be able to trust you again.

He closed his eyes, squeezing back the tears of grief and regret for all he'd thrown away by one careless act so long ago.

Where would they have been now if he hadn't gone to that party and ended up with Sue? Would they still have been together? He had no idea, but his track record wasn't great. Maybe he was so fundamentally flawed that he could never make a relationship work.

Well, he was going to make this one work, this friendship, if it killed him. He owed her that, at least. And maybe, in time, she'd learn that she could trust him again...

CHAPTER FIVE

SHE LAY AWAKE, listening for the sound of him coming up to bed, going over and over their conversation in her head. Could they do this? Really do it, put aside the huge sensual tug they both felt in favour of a straightforward friendship?

No. It was never going to be straightforward. Not with their history.

She heard his quiet tread on the stairs, the click of the light switch, the sound of running water and then silence. So near and yet so far...

It was hours before she went to sleep, and all too soon she was woken by a quiet tap on the door and Oliver's voice interrupting her dreams.

'Emily, it's six forty-five. What time does your shift start?'

Shift? She sat bolt upright and stared in horror at her alarm clock, then catapulted out of bed, heart pounding, and ran for the bathroom. She left the house five minutes later, arriving just after seven to find the department already busy.

If Oliver hadn't woken her… Then again, if he hadn't stayed, she wouldn't have had such a terrible night, and she certainly wouldn't have had those disturbing and unsettling dreams.

Would he still be there when she got home? No, of course not. She gave herself a mental shake, took a deep breath and joined the fray.

Kath went at three to catch her flight, and left Amelie in floods of tears. To her credit Kath had looked upset, too, but as long as she put her career first, this was always going to be the way of it.

He scooped his daughter up in his arms and hugged her as they went back inside and closed the door, and eventually she stopped sobbing and snuggled into his side on the sofa.

'So what would you like to do for the rest of the day?' he asked, and she shrugged, all forlorn.

'I don't know.'

'How about going to the beach?' he suggested to cheer her up. 'It's a nice day, and maybe we can get an ice cream?'

'Can I have a curly one with a chocolate stick in it?'

He ruffled her hair and smiled, happy to have his sunny little girl back. 'Sure, if we can find one. Let's go and see.'

He changed into shorts and trainers, found the bucket and spades, and they headed for the beach, and to his relief the stall was open and had the right sort of ice cream cone. Crisis averted. They sat down to eat them on the edge of the prom with their legs dangling, while the gulls swooped overhead, and when they were done, they took off their shoes, put them with the buckets and spades in a space on the beach and went down to the sea to wash their hands.

'It's freezing!' she shrieked, running and giggling back up the beach, and he followed her slowly, his heart aching for his little girl with her fractured life.

It wasn't all Kath's fault, either, however easy it was to blame her. He was busy, too, and it would have been career suicide to drop to part-time before he became a consultant. Maybe he could consider it now, so he had more time to share her precious childhood years? Or maybe both he and Kath could cut back a little? After all, compromise was a two-way street.

Like Emily, who was all about compromise,

making things work, putting her children front and centre of her life in a constant juggling act, and yet still trying to find a way to fit him into her hectic life. But only as a friend, which was more, really, than he had any right to ask…

He felt a sandy little hand grasp his and tug. 'Come on, Daddy, you have to help me. We're going to build the biggest sandcastle in the world!' Amelie said, and he put his emotional and physical needs on the back burner and knelt down next to his little daughter in the damp sand and reminded himself that this was what mattered, and all that could ever matter.

Monday was a bank holiday, so she'd taken the day off and spent it taming the garden, but Tuesday morning came all too soon.

She'd had to listen to the antics of Steve and Amanda's puppy all yesterday evening, and the begging and pleading was relentless.

'Phoebe, we can't have a dog, darling. You know we can't,' she'd said for the hundredth time as she tucked her up for the night, and then of course in the morning at school drop-off Elizabeth was there with Amelie and her little black dog, Berry, and Phoebe rushed over and cuddled it.

'Careful. You don't know her very well,' she warned, but Elizabeth smiled reassuringly.

'Don't worry, she's always fine with children. She loves them. How was your weekend?'

'Busy. I was working, apart from yesterday.' And apart from the time she was trying to seduce Elizabeth's son... 'How was yours?'

'Oh, lovely. Quiet. I went to my sister's, and we had a walk through Woodbridge and a coffee near the Tide Mill, then did some shopping. I actually found a new top that I like, which was the most exciting moment,' she added with a wry grin that reminded Emily so much of Oliver that her heart twisted in her chest.

She found a smile. 'Well, it sounds better than mine. I spent my weekend patching up DIYers and sports enthusiasts for the most part.' And having my feet massaged, and getting silly ideas about Oliver... 'Go on, in you go, Phoebe. Time to say goodbye,' she coaxed, and Phoebe kissed the dog on the nose and ran off to join the others.

'We should have another play date,' Elizabeth said. 'Come to ours. I'll bake us all a cake. How about tomorrow?'

She agreed on autopilot, and just hoped Oliver would be OK with it. He should be, it didn't affect him, but Amelie was his daughter, after all. He deserved a say in how much Emily was involved with her.

She told him in the first quiet moment, which wasn't until almost eleven. She found him in the staff kitchen washing down a sandwich with a glass of water, and he gave her a slightly wary smile.

'Hi. Everything OK?'

'Yes, fine,' she said, digging out an answering smile and wishing things could be different. 'Your mother's asked us round for another play date tomorrow. I just wanted to OK it with you.'

He gave her a puzzled frown. 'Of course it's OK. Why wouldn't it be?'

She shrugged. 'I don't know. It's your house, your daughter...'

'Emily, it's fine. I'm more than happy for Amelie to make friends with your children, and it's lovely that you and Mum are getting on so well. Really, I have no problem with it at all. You go for it.'

Except it didn't happen.

She turned up at school on Wednesday, and Elizabeth wasn't there. Amelie came out with the others, and she waited there with the three of them, but there was no sign of her. She tried Elizabeth's phone and it rang and rang and then went to voicemail, so she left a message and went to the office, but they hadn't heard from her, either.

'I'll call her,' the school secretary said, but Emily shook her head.

'Done that. She didn't answer. I'll try Amelie's father.'

She went back outside, scanning the road outside the playground, but still nothing, and then Oliver answered.

'Hi. What's up?'

'Do you know where your mother is?'

'My mother?' he said, sounding puzzled. 'She's with you, isn't she?'

'No. I'm at school with all the children, and there's no sign of her, and her phone went to voicemail. Do you want me to go to the house?'

'Uh—yeah, if you could? Take Amelie with you, and let me know as soon as you get there. Do you want me to come?'

'No. Don't worry, Oliver, she's probably just broken down somewhere without signal. She'll be fine. I'll call you when I know a bit more.'

'OK. I'll have my phone on me.'

He gave her the address, cleared it with the school, then they left and went straight to his house and found Elizabeth's car on the drive.

So where was she?

She turned and looked at the children. 'OK, stay here, all of you. I'll go and see where she is. I won't be long. She's probably just lost track of the time.' Or had an accident?

Elizabeth didn't answer the door, but she could hear the dog barking, and the door opened when she tried it, so she stepped inside.

'Elizabeth?'

Berry was running round her, then away again, and she heard a voice calling, so she followed the dog and found Elizabeth sitting on the blood-spattered kitchen floor in a sea of broken glass, clutching her right hand with her left.

'Oh, Emily, I'm so glad you've come,' she said, tearful with relief. 'Where are the children?'

'In the car. What have you done?' she asked gently, picking her way through the shards and then crouching down, her hand on Elizabeth's trembling shoulder.

'I've cut my palm. I slipped on some water and fell with a glass in my hand. So stupid. And I can't let go of it or it just bleeds and bleeds, and I could hear my phone ringing and there was nothing I could do. I couldn't get up without my hands, and I'm so worried Berry'll cut herself on the glass.'

'Right. Let's deal with that first, as you seem to have the bleeding under control,' she said calmly, 'and then we'll get you sorted out.' She straightened up and called Berry over to the bifold doors to the garden, checked her paws, then let her out before calling Oliver.

'I'm with your mother. She's cut her hand in the kitchen, so I'm going to bring her in, but I'll have all the children and I'll have to bring the dog because there's glass everywhere. Meet me at the door in ten minutes?'

'Sure. Is she OK?'

'She'll be fine,' she said reassuringly, not wanting to alarm either of them, then she swept the glass out of the way and smiled at Elizabeth.

'Right, we'd better take you to hospital and get that looked at,' she said, comforted that at least it wasn't still bleeding heavily, although from the look of her index finger she had some tendon damage.

She got Elizabeth up, shook the glass off her clothes and then wrapped her hand in a clean tea-towel, 'so we don't scare the children too much!', and led her out to the car and left Elizabeth explaining to the children while she ran back to pick up her bag, keys and the dog, and lock the door. She put Berry in the back, then jumped in the car and looked over her shoulder at the children.

'OK, everyone?'

Her two nodded, but Amelie looked wor-

ried. 'Are we taking Grandma to see Daddy?'
she asked.

'Yes, he's expecting us.' And hopefully he'd
be there.

To her relief he was, armed with a wheelchair, and Elizabeth shook her head.

'I don't need a wheelchair,' she protested,
but he just raised an eyebrow and helped her
into it, then turned to Emily, his eyes fraught
with worry.

'Could you be a star and take Amelie and
Berry back to yours?' he asked.

'I have a better idea. They were all expecting cake, so why don't I take them to the café,
and then we can take her home when she's
done? Berry can come with us.'

'That would be brilliant,' he agreed, and
stuck his head into the back of the car.

'Hi, Amelie. Hi, guys. I'm Amelie's dad,
and I'm just going to take my mum and get her
fixed, OK? You're going to stay with Emily
and I think there might be cake, if you're
good.'

'Will Grandma be all right, Daddy?'

Emily didn't hear his reply, just the gently reassuring tone of his voice, and then he
straightened up, gave her a fleeting smile and
wheeled his mother away.

Emily parked the car and led them round

the outside to the Park Café. 'Right. Let's have a look. What do you fancy, guys? Chocolate brownie, blueberry muffin, apple turnover, rocky road—'

She was drowned out by the chorus, so she started again, one by one, and loaded up the tray, picked up three cartons of juice and a coffee, and headed to a picnic bench.

'Right, here you are,' she said, and they settled down to munch their way through the cakes.

They were just finishing when her phone rang.

'Is that Daddy?' Amelie asked, looking a bit worried still, and Emily nodded and answered the call.

'Hi. How's it going?'

'OK, but she's going to need to stay in. She's done a proper job on it,' he told her, his voice stressed. 'It needs microsurgery and we can't do it down here. She's cut the tendon in her right index finger and severed a world of blood vessels, so we've put a compression dressing on it and she's going up to Theatre in a minute. I don't suppose there's any way you can take Amelie home with you until I finish work?'

'Of course I can,' she promised, and then handed the phone to Amelie who was desperate to talk to him.

'Is Grandma going to be all right?' she asked, and Emily could hear his voice cheerfully reassuring her, then telling her to give the phone back.

'All OK?' Emily asked.

'Yeah, I guess. I told her Grandma was very excited because she was going to have a sleepover here, and she'd be back home tomorrow. Not sure they need to know more than that for now.'

'OK. Well, come round when you're done and I'll feed them—not that they'll need a lot. They've eaten their body weight in cake.'

'No, I'm sure they won't. I've seen those cakes. Right, got to go. Take care. I'll come as soon as I can.'

'OK. No rush. We'll be fine.'

She hung up and turned back to the children.

'Well, that's exciting, Amelie, your grandma having a sleepover! I bet she wasn't expecting that! So Daddy wants you to come back to ours and he'll come when he's finished work, OK?'

'OK,' she said, but she still looked a bit worried.

'What's wrong?' she asked, and Amelie's eyes filled.

'She's not going to die, is she?'

Oh, bless her worried little heart. 'No, sweetheart, she's not going to die. She's just cut her hand!' she said reassuringly. 'They're going to mend her, and then she'll have a lovely rest and she can probably come home tomorrow.'

'Oh. That's OK, then. Can I have a sleepover, too?'

'I think we'll have to talk to Daddy about that,' she said, but it sounded like a good idea, because juggling the logistics was going to be tricky otherwise. 'Right, home, or shall we go to the playground first?'

It was well after seven before he arrived, and the children and Berry were lined up on the sitting room floor in front of the television, watching a film.

She saw the car pull up and went to the door, letting him in quietly.

'How is she? Did they fix the tendon?'

He shook his head. 'No, and it's not great. It was even worse than I thought. They've done the blood vessels, but the tendon damage is extensive and there's more than one involved, so they're operating tomorrow when the specialist hand surgeon's in. I just need to go home and grab her some things and take them back, and then I'll come and get Amelie.'

'And do what with her in the morning?' she asked gently.

He stared at her, gave a short sigh and dragged a hand over his face. 'Yeah. I don't know. I haven't thought that far ahead.'

'No, I'm sure you haven't. I have. Leave her here—she's already asked anyway. Go and get her things and your mum's, and some dog food, then come back and say goodnight to her. She'll be fine here and so will Berry.'

'Are you sure?'

'Of course I'm sure. She's totally up for it. They're watching a film right now, but it's nearly ended, so if you go quickly and come back with her things, you can spend a few minutes with her before you go back to the hospital.'

'And what do we do with Berry tomorrow? She can't spend your whole shift shut inside.'

'Leave it with me. James and Connie have dogs, so do Ryan and Beth, and so do Tom and Laura, and they're all in easy reach. One of them will have her, I'm sure.'

He hugged her briefly, mumbled, 'You're a star,' and went back out. Fifteen minutes later he was back, by which time she'd heated up his leftover chilli that she'd put in the freezer because she was sure he hadn't yet found time to eat.

'Sorry, you're eating,' he said, but she shook her head.

'I've eaten with the children. This is for you because I bet you haven't. Feed the dog while I dish it up.'

He sighed, a frustrated, unhappy sigh. 'Em, you didn't need to do this.'

'I know, but I work there, too, and I know how busy it gets. Plus I knew if you'd had a spare second, you would have been with your mother... It's not rocket science, and it's not exactly haute cuisine, either,' she added with a smile, and his mouth kicked up at one side, but it was a stressed, weary effort.

'Just eat,' she said gently. 'Tea, coffee, cold drink?'

He grunted. 'A glass of water would be great, but be careful with it,' he said with a wry grin. 'I've just cleared up the mess at home. She did a proper job, didn't she?'

'Yes, sorry, I had to leave it.'

'It's fine. I'm just grateful for all—'

'Yes, you've said that a thousand times,' she pointed out with a smile, and went to get his drink, putting water down for Berry while she was at it, and by the time she was back, he'd polished off the chilli. He wiped the plate with his bread and sat back with a weary smile.

'That was amazing. Thank you. Thank you for all of it—for finding her, for bringing her in, for looking after Amelie and Berry, for feeding me—I owe you big time.'

'Yes, you do,' she said, trying to keep a straight face. 'Don't worry, I'm keeping tabs on my brownie points. But you did make the chilli, so sadly it's not as big a tally as it could be.'

He chuckled and shook his head. 'You always were sassy,' he said softly, and then it was there again, that connection, the link between them that time had frayed but not severed.

'I haven't changed *that* much, Oliver,' she murmured, just as the film ended and Amelie got to her feet and ran over and hugged him, saving them from any further awkward conversations.

'How's Grandma?' Amelie asked, holding his face and staring into his eyes.

'She's OK. How are you? Are you still full of cake?'

'Up to here,' she said, holding her hand at nose level, and his eyes widened.

'*That* full? Wow. So how do you fancy a sleepover tonight with Billy and Phoebe?'

'Can I?' she asked, excitedly bouncing up and down, and he laughed and hugged her.

'I think that's a yes,' he said, and met Emily's eyes over her head. 'If Emily's OK with that?'

'Emily's very OK with that,' Emily said, and they all trooped upstairs. 'How about I put you in with Phoebe?' she suggested. 'She's got a pull-out bed you can have.'

'Cool. Can you read us a story, Daddy?'

He shook his head. 'No, darling, I'm sorry. I've got to take Grandma's stuff to her, but I'm sure Emily'll read to you.'

'Of course I will. Why don't you all get changed into your PJs and clean your teeth, and then we can find a book?'

He rang at nine thirty to see how she was coping, and they talked for a few minutes about his mother.

'I'm not sure how this is going to go. They're talking about her maybe needing to have it in a cast for several weeks while the tendons heal, if they have to graft them, so I have no idea how she's going to manage. She does so much for me. All the house stuff, the cooking, lots of the gardening, and she won't be able to drive. It's a nightmare.'

'I'm sure between us we can sort that out,' she said, trying to reassure him, but she heard his sigh and knew what he was going to say.

'You can't—'

'I can. Stop arguing and worrying, keep me posted if there's any news, and I'll see you in the morning after I've dropped Berry off with Laura and done the school run. And try and get some sleep, please?'

She heard a humourless huff of laughter, then another sigh. 'Fat chance,' he murmured, 'but thank you. I'll call you tomorrow.'

She put her phone down, put the dog out for a minute, then headed up to bed. The news hadn't been good, unlike the children who had been positively angelic for a change. Berry, though, was understandably unsettled, and she spent the night on Emily's bed for the sake of peace.

She dropped her off with Laura, then took the children to school. By the time she arrived at work, he'd spoken to the hand surgeon, and they were going to have to graft the tendons of Elizabeth's index and middle fingers.

'He's doing it this afternoon after his elective list, and he thinks it could be quite a long op, so she's going to be in for another night, and when she comes out, she won't be able to do anything. And as if it wasn't enough worrying about her and her recovery, I just don't know where to start with how I cope without her.' He raked his hands through his hair, stress written in capitals all over his face, and she laid a reassuring hand on his shoulder.

'You don't need to worry about that yet. I'll look after Amelie. One more is no harder, and I'm doing the school run anyway. We can do this, Oliver. We can manage. It's not a problem. You worry about your mother and leave the rest to me.'

'How? How can I do that? Amelie's hardly ever been away from me, and I tuck her up every night and wake her every morning, and that's if she doesn't wake in the night and come and get into bed with me. And it's not just her. What about the dog? I can't expect everyone to pick up the pieces for me.'

'So we'll find a dog walker for the days, and we'll live at yours for now,' she said calmly, although she wasn't at all sure how it would work. 'Assuming you've got enough space?'

'We've got tons of space, it's got four bedrooms and Mum's annexe, but that's not the point.'

'Yes, it is, and I'm sure we'll cope,' she said, as much to herself as to him, and then looked around. 'So, where do I need to be first?'

'With me in Resus? And this conversation isn't finished, just so you know. We can talk later when I get home.'

'I'll need keys.'

'There's a key safe by the door. I'll send you the code.'

By the end of her shift Elizabeth's operation was under way, she'd spoken to a dog walker who sounded as if she might be able to help, and she went home with all the children and Berry, and sat them down and asked them how they felt about going to stay at Amelie's house for a few days.

Billy and Phoebe were ridiculously excited, but Amelie looked worried.

'Isn't Grandma coming back?' she asked, and Emily reassured her hastily.

'Of course she's coming back, sweetheart, but her hand is a bit poorly, so she won't be able to do very much, so we're all going to have to help her. That's all it is, and we can do that, can't we? Make her life a little bit easier?'

They all nodded, and she smiled at them and mentally crossed her fingers that it would really be that easy. 'Great. Right, we need to pack some things!'

By the time he finished his shift at seven, his mother was in Recovery, and he ran up to see her, then left her in the care of the surgical team and drove home. Not for long, he'd have to go back, but he had to be there for Amelie, and he had no idea how Emily was coping.

Brilliantly, as it turned out. He opened the front door and was greeted by Berry and the wonderful smell of something delicious. He followed the sound of the children's voices and found them in the kitchen sitting at the table in their pyjamas, heads bent over their drawings.

Emily was standing at the stove, her hair scraped back into a messy ponytail with the odd escaping wisp, and she turned and smiled at him, her eyes searching as she mouthed, 'OK?'

He nodded and went over to the table, laying a hand on Amelie's shoulder, and she looked up at him and reached up her arms.

'Daddy! How's Grandma?'

'She's fine,' he said, stretching the truth as he bent and hugged her. 'She's very, very sleepy, but she's going to be fine. Her hand's all mended now and it just has to finish getting better, but that's going to take a long, long time, so we'll have to look after her, OK?'

She nodded. 'Emily said we were going to help her,' she told him, and then wriggled out of his arms and picked up a sheet of paper with a drawing of...

'Is that Grandma?' he asked, looking at the

picture of a person with a humungous bandage on one very oversized arm.

'Yes. And that's blood,' she said, all matter-of-fact, pointing to a red splodge on her bandage. 'Emily's cooking you a surprise,' she said, her eyes theatrically wide. 'You'll never guess what it is.'

He knew exactly what it was, because paella had been her signature dish all those years ago, just as chilli had been his, and anyway even if he couldn't smell it, the pan was a dead giveaway.

'Um—fish pie?'

She shook her head.

'I know! Frog's legs on toast.'

That made her giggle, and he saw Emily's shoulders shake as she tried not to laugh.

'OK, one last guess. Um…cauliflower cheese?'

'No. See, I told you you'd never guess,' she said triumphantly, and picked up the crayons again.

He met Emily's eyes again over their heads and smiled.

'Is there anything you need me to do?'

'Yes. I need you to sit down and chill for a minute. Drink?'

'Don't worry, I'll get something. I've got to go back and see Mum later, after I've put

Amelie to bed and eaten whatever it is you're cooking up over there.'

He winked at her, and she smiled an enigmatic smile and went back to her pan, and he got a glass of water from the fridge dispenser and perched on a stool at the island, watching her cook as he had so many times before. She lifted the lid, testing the grains of rice, adding a spoonful of stock, before covering it again.

'Is it done?'

'Not quite. Right, children, I reckon it's time to clear up the table and head upstairs to bed, don't you? Oliver, maybe you need to come and make sure everyone's in the right rooms.'

'Whatever you've done will be fabulous,' he said, 'just so long as we've all got a bed to lie on. Come on, guys, you can show me where you're sleeping.'

It was after eight before the children were all settled and they were able to eat, and almost half past ten by the time Oliver got back from the hospital.

She knew the second his car pulled up on the drive, because Berry was up off the sofa and straight to the front door, tail wagging furiously.

He gave her a quick stroke, then walked into the sitting room with a weary smile.

'Hi. Everything all right?'

'It's fine, all quiet. I want to hear about your mother,' she said, and he let out a long, slow sigh and shook his head.

'She's OK. She's a tiny bit sore, so they upped her pain meds and she's sleepy now, which is a good thing, but she's worried, which isn't.'

'About her hand?'

'No. Not at all. She hardly mentioned it and I'm not sure she's understood the significance of it long-term. No, she's worried about us— about me having to cope without her, about you taking on so much, about Billy and Phoebe being uprooted—all of it, really.'

'Did you reassure her?'

He laughed, a soft, hollow huff, his eyes closing and his head tipping back.

'I tried, but I agree with everything she said. She's indispensable, and while she loves to be needed, she's really angry with herself for daring to have an accident.'

'That sounds pretty typical. She's always put everyone else first.' She studied him, lying there with his eyes shut, looking shattered. 'Do you want me to get you a drink?'

He sat up. 'No, you're fine. I'll get one. How about you? Fancy a glass of wine? I reckon we've both earned it.'

She smiled slowly. 'Yes, I think I do, actually. Only one. I can't stay up too late, but I'll have one with you.'

He disappeared for a moment, then came back and sat down at the other end of the sofa, but it wasn't a big one and Berry was between them, so it was…cosy, to say the least.

Cosy, and intimate, and just a teeny bit dangerous for her peace of mind.

He shifted slightly and turned so he was facing her a little, his arm along the back of the sofa, fingers just inches from her shoulder, and smiled a little sadly.

'I can't get over what you've done for us, yesterday and today. I don't know where to start to thank you. I'm just so ridiculously beholden to you.'

'Well, what can I say? Just look at all those brownie points I'm clocking up.'

'I am. Right now it's looking like I owe you two months on a tropical island, lying under a banana-leaf shelter, sipping a hideous blue cocktail rammed with ice with a ludicrous umbrella stuck in the top of it, while your personal beautician finishes your foot massage and pedicure.'

She closed her eyes and leaned her head back with a happy sigh.

'Keep talking. I can hear the waves breaking on the shore, and smell the sea. I might even go diving tomorrow from a boat, if I can be bothered. Or I might just have another foot massage.'

He chuckled, and she felt him shift and the warm weight against her side lifted as Berry was hoisted off the sofa.

'Feet,' he said, putting his wine down and beckoning, and she swung them round and rested them on his lap, closing her eyes again with a groan of ecstasy as his fingers got to work.

'See, I don't need to go to a tropical island,' she said lazily. 'I can just lie here like this and pretend.'

She'd fallen asleep.

He sat sipping his wine and watched her— not for long, not really, because he needed to go to sleep soon himself, but long enough that the urge to scoop her into his arms and carry her up to bed was almost overwhelming.

No. Not appropriate. He didn't need to mess with the fragile status quo before the meta-phorical ink on her generous offer of help was even dry. And anyway, there were three kids in the house who'd be a mess of questions if they got caught.

He shifted her feet, lifting them gently and

sliding out from under them, threw her wine, virtually untouched, down the sink and put both glasses in the dishwasher, then went back and sat beside her and laid a hand on her shoulder.

'Hey, sleepy-head. It's time for bed,' he said softly, and she stirred and opened her eyes.

'Oh. Sorry. Long day.'

'Tell me about it,' he said, dredging up what might pass for a smile. 'You go on up. I'll sort the dog out. I'll be up in a minute.'

She nodded and got to her feet, and he watched her go, an ache in his chest. How long could he expect her to help him out? She'd stepped up without a thought for herself, taken over where his mother had left off and done it all with a smile.

He really, really didn't deserve that. Not after the way it had all ended, which had been pretty much all his fault. He'd let her down, lost her trust for ever, and yet here she was, playing the good Samaritan and bailing him out.

He couldn't let her do it indefinitely, but for now he had little choice. He'd just make sure she realized how grateful he was, and maybe somehow return the favour.

He got to his feet with a heavy sigh. 'Come on, Berry, time for bed. You need to go out,' he said, and headed for the door.

CHAPTER SIX

ELIZABETH WAS DISCHARGED the following day, and Oliver took the afternoon off and drove her home.

She was exhausted, and even though she denied it, he could see she was in a certain amount of pain, but she seemed glad to be home.

'You need a rest,' he said, and she nodded. She even allowed him to take off her dress, the only button-through thing he'd been able to find in her wardrobe, but she drew the line at her underwear.

He lifted back the duvet so she could get into bed, and as she turned, he could see bruises coming out all over the place from her fall. He sorted her pillows, covered her up and fetched her a glass of water to put by the bed, and she eyed it ruefully.

'That's what got me into this mess,' she said, and he smiled.

'Just don't get out of bed with it,' he said, and kissed her cheek. 'You have a sleep. I'll see you in a bit. Call if you need me—your phone's right here. Berry, come on, Grandma doesn't need you on her bed.'

'She's fine,' she said, reaching out her good hand and stroking her loyal little friend. 'Leave her here. She's good company.'

'OK. You know where I am.'

He left her to it and walked back into the main house, leaving the door ajar so he could hear her.

He had about half an hour before Emily would be here with the children. And they'd be here all weekend, which wasn't really necessary and would add to the noise, which might tire his mother. Unless she wasn't planning to stay for the weekend? As neither of them were working again until Monday, there was no need to, and she was doing more than enough anyway.

Still, as she'd said, it was only temporary, and there would be no need for her to be here at all once he could find a temporary replacement for his mother. He really needed to get on that. He picked up his phone, but he'd hardly started to look for au pairs when he heard a car on the drive. He closed his mother's door softly, and went to let them in.

Time for a conversation…

The front door opened before they reached it, and Oliver let them in with a finger pressed to his lips.

'Grandma's having a rest,' he murmured, 'so if you could all be really quiet, that would be very helpful.'

'Is she OK?' Amelie whispered, and he nodded.

'She is, but she's tired.'

'Can I see her?'

'Not till she wakes up, but I'm sure she'll be delighted to see you then.'

Emily met his eyes over their heads, and she raised an eyebrow questioningly.

'Everything OK?'

He nodded. 'Yeah. Fine. She's just getting over the anaesthetic.'

She wasn't convinced. 'Why don't we settle the children down with a drink and a biscuit in front of the TV,' she suggested. That way she could find out what was wrong, because something clearly was.

They left them in the sitting room watching cartoons and migrated back to the kitchen, and she turned to face him.

'So what's up?' she asked softly.

'Nothing—well, not with her, but as neither of us are working now till Monday morning, I think there's no real need for you to be here over the weekend. Mum's quite tired and bruised and a little shaken up, so some peace and quiet wouldn't go amiss, but if you think that's too disruptive for the kids—'

She shook her head. 'No, that's fine. I was thinking the same thing myself, so long as you're sure you can cope?'

'Of course I can cope.'

'Good. So what else is bothering you? Because it's not just that.'

He scrubbed a hand through his hair and sighed. 'You. Well, no, not you, just—I'm putting on you, so I've been doing some research, and I'm going to get an au pair.'

She frowned. 'I thought we'd had this conversation?'

'We have, but realistically I can't expect you to do this indefinitely. When you offered, we were talking short-term, but her injury is worse than we'd thought and it's going to be weeks—months—before she's properly up and running again, and if I don't get someone in to cover for her, she'll be overdoing it, and I know perfectly well she will, whatever I say. She's stubborn.'

'Well, that runs in the family,' she said bluntly. 'So what did you find out?'

He shrugged. 'Not much, I've only just started looking, but I'm so conscious of the massive disruption to your lives. And I know you're going to argue, but it's not fair on you and it's not fair on the children, so I need to sort this.'

There was more to it than that, but she let it go. For now. 'OK. By all means look, but really, we're fine. This makes sense for everybody, especially for Amelie, and yes, it's disruptive, yes, it's not ideal, but does she really need to be looked after by a total stranger?'

'But my mother would be here.'

'And she would feel she had to help, which could be awkward. For goodness' sake, Oliver, just accept my help. It's not for ever. Unless you really don't want us here?'

He held her eyes, something unreadable in his, then looked away. 'It's not that. Not that at all. I just feel guilty.'

'Well, don't. It's fine. We'll go home this weekend, which I'd planned to do anyway. It'll give your mother more peace and quiet to get over the anaesthetic, and there are lots of things I need to do, like pack a few more things, do the washing, sort out the fridge, cut the grass—life stuff,' she said with a smile, and he gave a soft huff of laughter and returned her smile.

'Thank you. And it's not that you aren't welcome, it's not that I don't want you here—'

She took a step forward and put a finger over his lips, stopping him in mid-sentence.

'Oliver, it's OK,' she murmured. 'I understand, and it's fine. I'll take them home, sort out my house, and we'll see you on Sunday evening, shall we, after supper?'

'Come earlier,' he said. 'I'll cook for us all.'

'If you're sure?'

He nodded slowly. 'I'm sure. Of course I'm sure. It's the least I can do under the circumstances, and I'll get another solution as soon as I can.'

'Don't be silly,' she said. 'You look after your mum, and we'll come back on Sunday and we'll see how it goes from there.'

Emily and the children went, and the house felt weirdly empty. He reminded himself that that was a good thing, because his mother needed quiet, but it still felt somehow wrong.

His mother woke a little later and called him, and he tapped on the door and went in, to find her sitting on the edge of the bed looking helpless.

'I can't get dressed,' she said crossly, and

he could tell she was on the verge of tears. That shocked him, because his mother never, ever cried. Well, that wasn't quite true. There'd been a lot of crying when his father died, but since then she'd just soldiered on. Maybe for too long...

He sat down on the bed beside her and put his arm round her shoulders. 'It's OK. I can help you.'

'You can't. Not really, not enough. I must have hurt my left wrist as well when I fell, and I've been lying here thinking about it, and there are all sorts of things I'm not going to be able to do for myself. I can't even make a cup of tea, because I can't lift a kettle with either hand, and anyway there's all the personal stuff, like getting washed and dressed.'

'I can help—'

'No! Oliver, you can't,' she said, her voice firming up. 'I know you're a doctor, I know you've seen it all, but you haven't seen *mine*, and you're not going to. You're my son, not my doctor, not my carer. Can you ask Emily to come and help me, please?'

He sighed quietly. He hadn't anticipated this at all. Perhaps he should have done. 'She's not here.'

'Not here?'

'No. She's gone home with the children for the weekend. I told her we could manage.'

'Well, I can't, apparently, and you aren't going to do those things for me and that's an end to it.'

'So what do you suggest?' he asked, feeling totally blindsided by this, because he really, really hadn't thought it through.

'I'm going to ring Catherine.'

'Catherine?'

'Yes, Catherine. My sister. Your aunt.'

'I know perfectly well who you're talking about, Mum, but what are you suggesting? That she comes and stays here?'

'No. I'm going to ask if I can go and stay with her for a few weeks. I'm sure she'll say yes, and it'll give me some company in the day.'

'*Weeks?* Really?'

'Well, why not? She's alone, I'm alone, she's got a garden suitable for Berry, she can walk her—I don't see what's wrong with it. Emily will have enough to do without worrying about me and the dog, and anyway, she won't be here in the day so what happens then?'

He frowned. 'It might not be Emily.'

'What do you mean? You said she was going to stay here and take over from me for a little while.'

'She is—she was, but it's a heck of an imposition, and I assumed you'd be here, so I was thinking of getting an au pair. She could help you, just until your other wrist is better.'

She frowned. 'Never mind about me, I don't matter, but are you saying you're going to get a total stranger to look after Amelie while you're at work?' She laid her hand on his knee. 'Poor little thing. Don't you think she's had enough change and disruption in her little life without that? She's got to know Emily, she knows the children, it's all familiar—how is a stranger possibly better?'

Because I won't have Emily getting under my skin at home as well as at work. It's already impossible to think straight.

'I don't want to take advantage of her—and I can help you.'

She gave him a level look and got to her feet with difficulty. 'We're not going over that again, Oliver. Could you please help me put my dress on? And then I'd love a cup of tea. You can make it while I phone Catherine. And don't argue.'

He didn't. It was pointless, so he did as he was asked, and the tea was waiting for her in the kitchen when she emerged. He could hear her in the sitting room talking to Amelie, so he picked up the tea and went through, and found them snuggled up together on the sofa.

He removed Berry who was lying sprawled across them both, and put the tea down beside her.

'Thank you, darling. I've spoken to Catherine. She's coming over in the morning to collect me,' she said, and picked up the tea with a little wince.

He opened his mouth, met her eyes across the top of the mug and shut it. He'd seen that look enough times in his life to know what it meant. It didn't solve all his problems, though, because he really, really didn't want to have to rely on Emily, but he still hadn't got the slightest idea what else he could do.

He picked up his phone, and while Amelie spent the next half hour decorating her grandmother's cast with felt-tip pens and a running commentary, he scrolled through all manner of websites about au pairs. There were lots of comments, too, some singing their praises, and others outlining the perils and pitfalls.

OK, they were few and far between, but what if the person he chose was a disaster? What if Amelie wasn't safe? How could he know if he could trust a stranger with his precious child?

He couldn't. And his mother was right—

she'd had enough change in her short life and at least he knew he could trust Emily implicitly. He'd just have to keep his mind and his body under control.

His heart, well, that was another matter. It was already a lost cause.

Emily spent the weekend blitzing the house and the garden, doing the washing and packing up the things they'd need for the next week.

Clothes were a bit of an issue. The children got through them at such a rate, and Phoebe had shot up and outgrown most of her summer clothes. All last year's dresses were too short, her favourite dungarees weren't long enough in the body, and Billy wasn't much better off.

She could always wash them at Oliver's, she supposed—or run back here and do them after Oliver was home and the children were in bed?

Or she could go and buy more, so she had enough to last a week at a time. That made sense.

She took them to the supermarket, found a few things which fitted and which they didn't hate, then loaded up the car and went back to Oliver's at five.

She rang the bell, and he let them in with a puzzled frown.

'What's wrong with your key?'

'I didn't want to presume—'

'Don't be ridiculous, Em. You're living here! Treat it as your home, please?'

'But it isn't— OK, OK! Sorry. How's your mother?'

The children ran in, looking for Amelie and Berry, and he rolled his eyes and stifled a laugh. 'Stubborn and awkward. She's gone to her sister's with the dog.'

Emily felt her eyes widen, and her heart gave a sudden thump. 'Really? For how long?'

'Really. And—weeks, she said, until she can manage her personal care. She wouldn't let me do anything even remotely personal for her. I didn't realize it, but she'd hurt her left wrist as well, so doing anything was difficult, and apparently I'm her son and some things are out of bounds.'

Her mouth twitched and she bit her lips. 'OK.'

'Don't laugh at me. It just hadn't occurred to me that she'd be so…'

'Protective of her privacy?'

He laughed at that. 'I was going to say coy, but—yeah. She asked for you. I had to explain you'd gone home. And I told her I was going to find an au pair.'

'And how's that going?' she asked, sensing it wasn't good.

He shook his head and turned away. 'Come into the kitchen while I cook. The kids are OK. They're in the garden and we can see them from there. They can't come to much harm.'

She climbed onto a stool at the island and watched him thoughtfully, her mind assimilating the fact that without Elizabeth here the evenings were going to be…interesting, to say the least. 'So—the au pair thing.'

'Yeah. It's a minefield. I've been trawling the advice threads. Some au pairs are amazing, some not—oh, and some are man-eaters.'

That made her really laugh. 'You are rather making the assumption that they'd *want* to seduce you,' she said, trying not to think too much about him being seduced, but he just rolled his eyes.

'Whatever. I can cope with a hormonal teenager—that's the least of my worries. What I'm worried about is my daughter, her safety, her emotional security. How will she feel being looked after by a total stranger? She's been through enough and right now everything's new—the school, the house—she doesn't need this.'

She stifled a smile. 'Well, you know what I think,' she said, and resisted the urge to say, 'I told you so'.

'Yes, I do know, and for now at least I have

very little choice but to accept your help with Amelie, but I'm not happy about it.'

She got up, walked round the island and put a hand over his mouth. 'Oliver, shut up and cook the supper, and stop beating yourself to death over it. It's temporary. Cope with it.'

'OK, OK,' he mumbled, and she felt his lips pucker as he kissed her hand, his lips soft and warm and slightly moist against her skin.

Their eyes locked, and she dropped her hand as if his mouth was red-hot and turned away. This had suddenly got a whole lot more complicated...

'So what are you cooking?' she asked, hoping her voice didn't really sound quite so strangled as it felt.

'A one-pot chicken recipe of Mum's. It's easy, Amelie eats it and it's reasonably healthy.'

'Sounds like a win. Are you serving it with pasta?'

His lips quirked. 'No. I'm not. I'm serving it with peas and new potatoes. Will they eat that?'

'My kids? They'll eat anything, Billy especially.' And then, just because it was getting really hard to sit in there and watch him, she added, 'How long before we eat? Have I got time to bring the stuff in from the car?'

He glanced at the clock. 'Ten minutes? The chicken's ready. I've just got to do the veg.'

'Great. I'll do it now,' she said, and escaped from the kitchen with a tingling hand, a silent sigh of relief and a vow never, ever to touch him again.

The week started well, considering.

Work was busy but not horrendously so, and the children seemed to be getting on OK, which was a massive relief to him as Amelie could be tricky sometimes with her friendships. But on a personal level, it was an exercise in frustration and denial.

It was fine until the children were all in bed, but then they were left alone together. They didn't have to be. He could have taken himself off to his study, she could have gone in his mother's rooms and made herself at home, or he could, but without fail they ended up on the sofa listening to music, watching the TV, reading—and all the time his senses were filled by her.

Every move, every breath, every drift of the scent of her body, every page she turned registered. And if they talked the conversation was either artificial or straying into dangerous territory, and the last thing he wanted was to rehash all the might-have-beens, so he held it together and kept telling himself it wasn't for ever.

And then on Thursday his run of luck at work ran out, with the day from hell, and it all fell apart.

It was late by the time Oliver got home.

He stuck his head into the kitchen, and she took one look at his face and knew it wasn't good.

'Are the children in bed?' he asked, and she nodded.

'Long ago. I told Amelie you'd come in and say goodnight, but I haven't heard a sound.'

'OK. I need a shower anyway.'

She was standing in the kitchen with her back to him when he came down a few minutes later, and she heard his quiet tread as he walked over to her.

'I'm sorry I was so late. Do you need a hand?' he asked, but there was something in his voice that troubled her, and she turned her head and smiled at him, but his face was expressionless.

'No, you're fine.'

Except he wasn't fine.

She switched off the hob and turned back to him, and for a fleeting second his eyes were unguarded, raw and touched with pain.

'Tough day?' she asked gently.

He closed his eyes and nodded, and she reached out for him. 'Come here,' she murmured, and he walked into her arms and stood there, his head resting against hers, and she sensed his body was held up by sheer willpower.

'Want to talk about it?'

He shook his head, just the tiniest movement, and then opened his eyes and stared into hers.

For a moment they just stood there, and then his lips were on hers, his kiss wild and a little desperate. She understood, because this wasn't about them, it was about him, and as his hands cupped her face, his mouth urgent, his body taut, she held him and kissed him back as the storm raged through him.

And then finally she felt the tension go out of him, and the kiss slowed and gentled, his hands cradling her head tenderly as he stroked his lips against hers, the damp skin clinging before he pulled away.

'Sorry, I don't know what that was all about,' he said gruffly, his voice echoing with sadness, but she did, and she touched his cheek in comfort.

'Tell me,' she coaxed.

He shook his head and moved away a fraction, but she pulled him back, and he rested his head against hers with a slow, heavy sigh.

'Her name was Helena. She was just a kid. Twelve. She was knocked off her bike on the way home from school, and she didn't make it. Telling her parents was the hardest thing I've ever done.' His eyes squeezed shut. 'How does that feel? To be her parents? To know she's never coming home again? How will they do that, Em? How will they go on?'

A tear slid down his cheek, and she kissed it away.

'I have no idea. I'm so sorry, Oliver.'

'Don't. You should be sorry for them, not me.'

'Why not you, too? I know what it's like. They all say, don't get involved, and when you're working you don't, but when it's done and you walk away, then it all comes crashing back and of course it hurts, because we're human, and we care, or we wouldn't be doing the job, and every one we lose stays with us for ever.'

'I can't get her out of my head. I want to forget, but she's just there, even when I close my eyes. I wanted to save her, Emily, and I couldn't. I failed her.'

'No, you didn't. Sometimes you just can't save them, but you saved Jack—he's in a rehab centre now to carry on his recovery, and without you he would be dead for sure.'

'You would have done what I did.'

'Maybe, maybe not. But it was you who did it. Not me.'

'We all did it.'

'We did, and we do it every day, and we win some, we lose some, and today, you lost, but tomorrow there'll be someone else you save who would have died.'

He nodded slowly, then moved away from her, and she missed his warmth—not the physical warmth, but the warmth of his compassion, his caring, his empathy, the things that made him Oliver, made him the man she'd loved. Still loved, if only she could trust him…

'So what are you cooking?' he asked gruffly, and she dredged out a smile.

'Chicken and mushroom stroganoff, with tenderstem broccoli and wild rice.'

She turned back to the stove, and she heard the scrape of a stool on the floor as he sat down at the island.

'Anything I can do?' he asked, and she shook her head.

'Not really. I'm almost done. You could get some cutlery out and a couple of glasses of cold water while I dish up.'

She put the plate down in front of him and slid onto another stool, and he picked up his fork.

'Were the kids OK after school?'

'Yes, they were fine. They're lovely together. They spent ages in the garden making a little den behind the Portuguese laurel in the corner, and they took some of Amelie's toy kitchen stuff out there and made a campfire and "cooked" on it.'

The smile just about reached his eyes. 'Did you have to eat it?'

'Oh, yes. Frogspawn and toadstool curry, they told me. Apparently they were fairies.'

His mouth twitched, and this time the smile really did reach his eyes. 'I'm glad you didn't cook that for us. I eat pretty much anything, but I might have had to draw the line at that.'

She smiled back. 'You're not alone. Even pretending was hard!'

He laughed, but then his smile faded, and he frowned.

Back in that dark place.

'Talk to me.'

He shook his head slowly. 'Helena's parents. They couldn't understand why she was dead. There was hardly a mark on her, but she started fitting, and her pupils blew, and I couldn't do anything about it. She must have had a massive traumatic brain injury.'

'How long was she with you?'

'Not long. Twenty minutes? And she was OK at first, then—I just keep seeing her parents, the look in their eyes. And I know there was nothing I could do, I'm not stupid, but even so—they were relying on me to save her, and I couldn't.'

He pushed his plate away, and she pushed it back.

'Eat. Now. And then we'll go and sit down and you can talk about it for as long as you need, but just so you know, you didn't fail anyone, and it's not your fault. Eat.'

He knew she was right, and his body was hungry, so he ate, and then they went and curled up on the sofa together, and gradually the warmth of her body against his side began to penetrate the icy wall around his heart.

He felt a tear slide down his cheek, then another, and she wiped them away with gentle fingers.

'How will they cope?' he asked.

'How does anyone cope with loss, Oliver? It's hard. One foot in front of the other, I guess.'

Was that how she'd coped when he'd told

her about Sue? Not that it was the same, but it had obviously hurt her very deeply. He could imagine that. It had hurt him, too, even though it had been his fault. And now, despite that hurt, she was here for him.

'Thank you,' he said quietly, and she turned her head and looked up at him.

'What for?'

He shrugged. 'Being here for me? Talking me down off a cliff—'

'A cliff?'

He shook his head and smiled. 'No, not that cliff. I just felt like I was standing on the edge of a deep black hole, and you pulled me back away from it. You and your calm common sense and unquestioning kindness. Your warmth, your generosity...'

He trailed off, because the next step was to tell her he loved her, and he couldn't do that. Not yet, and maybe never. She didn't want to hear it, and he knew he had a long way to go to win back her trust.

He eased his arm out from behind her and stood up.

'I think I'm going to turn in.'

'Are you OK now?' she asked, her eyes worried, and he nodded.

'Yes, I'm fine. It happens to all of us, but yeah, I'm fine. Thank you. Again.'

He pulled her to her feet, wrapped his arms round her and hugged her. 'It's good having you here,' he said into her hair, and then he dropped his arms and stepped away before he did anything stupid like kiss her again, because this time it really wouldn't end there.

To his amazement he slept well, and Friday was fine. No drama, no tragedy for a change, just the usual stuff.

And then Kath came for the weekend, while Steve had Emily's children and she was at work, and while he cut the lawn, Amelie came out into the garden and played in the den she'd made with Billy and Phoebe.

'Why aren't you with Mummy?' he asked as he finished, and she told him Mummy was working. He gritted his teeth, put the mower away and went inside, leaving her playing in the den. Time to deal with this.

Half an hour later, after a fairly blunt conversation with Kath, he ran upstairs, packed a bag and went out into the garden to talk to Amelie in her new den.

'I've got to go somewhere, sweetheart, but Mummy's going to do something lovely with you, OK? I'll see you tomorrow.'

'Are you going to work?' she asked.

'No, but I have to go away and see someone.

I'm sorry. I'll be back tomorrow, but you have fun with Mummy, OK?'

'OK.' She hugged him, lifted up her face for a kiss and then ran inside. He could hear her excited voice, asking her mother what they were going to do, and he bit his lips, wondering if tough love would work or if it would bring it all crashing down on their heads.

Only one way to find out. He went back in and found Kath sitting with Amelie, discussing options. Good.

'Bye, guys. See you tomorrow. Have fun,' he said, and kissed his daughter goodbye and left before he changed his mind.

His car was on her drive when she got home, but there was no sign of him and the key was still under the pot, so she rang him.

'Where are you? What's going on?'

He gave a strangled laugh. 'Yeah, Kath and I had a bit of a frank conversation about her priorities, and told her I'd see her tomorrow.'

'Wow. OK. So where are you now?'

'On the clifftop. The café closed so I had to leave, and I didn't like to presume and let myself in.'

'Don't be ridiculous. You can come here whenever you like. I'm all over your house, for heaven's sake. Are you staying the night?'

'If I can? Otherwise, I'll go to a hotel.'

'Don't be ridiculous. Come back now. I'm not doing anything, and you sound as if you need to talk.'

Five minutes later he walked in the door, and she gave him a quick hug and went into the kitchen before she forgot her common sense and stayed in his arms. It was becoming a dangerous habit.

'What do you fancy for supper?' she asked, wondering if there was anything in the freezer that she could throw together, apart from pizzas and the odd bag of frozen peas.

'How about going out again like we did before?' he said, his voice close behind her. 'You've been cooking for us all week, you've been working all day—I reckon you've earned it.'

She hesitated, then turned and nodded. 'OK. Give me ten minutes to shower and change?'

'Sure. I need to ring Amelie and say goodnight anyway, so no rush.'

She didn't rush, because somehow this time it mattered more. She went casual again, but prettier and cooler, in the new floaty floral dress she'd picked up the other day when she'd shopped for the children. She put on sandals and picked up a lightweight cardi in case they sat outside, and ran down.

He was standing at the patio doors staring out at the garden, a jumper knotted casually over his shoulders, and he turned to her with a smile.

'You look nice. Your grass needs cutting, by the way.'

'Feel free. You can earn back some brownie points,' she said, oddly flustered by his compliment. 'How was Amelie?'

'Fine, I think. They seem to have had fun. I think they spent some time on the beach and went to a café for supper, luckily not the one I was in. Which brings me to us. Any suggestions?'

'There's a lovely pub on the river someone was talking about the other day, with fabulous views and lots of outside space. Fancy trying that?'

'Why not? It's a gorgeous evening. We can sit outside.'

It was gorgeous, absolutely gorgeous, and they stayed until the sun was long gone and she was feeling the chill even through her cardi.

'You're cold. Here, have my jumper,' he said, pulling it off, and she slipped it over her head and was engulfed in an intoxicating mixture of laundry soap and Oliver.

She tugged it down and smiled at him. 'Thanks.'

'You're welcome. Another drink?'

'No, I don't think so. How about a stroll to the end of the jetty?'

It was magical by the water, the lights from the boats moored out on the river glinting on the surface, the smell of the riverbank in every breath.

They lingered a little, but all she could think about was how nice it would be if he put his arm around her and hugged her against his side so she could rest her head on his shoulder as she had the other night...

Bad idea.

'The wind's picking up,' she said with a little shiver. 'Let's go back.'

They drove home, and as soon as they walked in the door, she headed for the stairs. 'I'll just change Billy's sheets—'

'You don't need to do that. I can do it later. Come down.'

She turned on the stairs and walked down, and as she reached the bottom step, she met his eyes and something happened, something hot and sweet and irresistible that stopped them both in their tracks.

He closed his eyes and turned away with a sharp sigh. 'I shouldn't be here. This was a bad idea,' he muttered, and she sat down, partly because her legs were shaking and partly because she didn't trust herself not to walk down and wrap her arms around him.

She wrapped them round herself instead, and watched him. His head was bowed, and she could hear the cogs turning, feel the inward battle he was waging with his emotions.

She recognized that battle. It was with her day and night, but the wanting was killing her and the need to hold him was stronger than her resolve.

'Oliver?'

He lifted his head and turned towards her, keeping the bannisters between them.

'I shouldn't be here,' he said again, but she could hear the lack of resolution in his voice this time, the sound of surrender to the inevitable that echoed in her heart.

'Shouldn't you?' she asked softly. 'Are you sure?'

He was silent for so long she was starting to doubt her own judgement, but then he met her eyes again, and she could see tenderness and longing in them. She stood up and took the last step down as he rounded the bannisters and reached for her, and as she went into his arms it felt as if she was coming home.

He held her eyes for another heartbeat, then

lowered his head and kissed her, his lips brushing hers lightly, tentatively, questioningly.

It was nothing like the other night. This kiss was all about them, him rediscovering her as she was rediscovering him?

She took a step back out of his arms, slid her hand into his and led him wordlessly up to her room.

CHAPTER SEVEN

HE TURNED HER to face him, and she could feel the tremor in his hands as he cupped her shoulders.

She hadn't put the light on, but there was a full moon and she could make out his features, the set of his lips as he pressed them together, the questioning tilt of his head as he stared down into her eyes, and when he spoke, his voice was gruff.

'If we do this, we can't turn back the clock and undo it.'

'I won't want to undo it,' she told him, and something in her voice must have convinced him, because he gave a tiny nod of recognition and she saw his throat move as he swallowed.

His hands reached down, finding the hem of his borrowed jumper and peeling it slowly over her head. He dropped it on the floor and eased the cardi over her shoulders, before letting it slide to the floor with the jumper, and then he studied the dress.

'How does that come off?' he asked, and she bent and grasped the hem and pulled it over her head.

She heard the intake of his breath, the silence that followed, and she added the dress to the growing pile on the floor and reached for his shirt buttons, undoing them slowly one by one with fingers that trembled.

His breath hissed out but he stood motionless, his hands warm and firm as they cupped her shoulders, his fingers tightening as she reached for the stud on his jeans. She tugged the shirt out and slid it off his shoulders, and he shrugged it off, then reached for his zip.

She slapped his hands away gently and took over, and as her fingers grazed down over his abdomen, it tensed, and she felt him shudder.

'You're killing me, you know that, don't you?' he murmured, and bending his head he nuzzled into the side of her neck above her collarbone, his breath warm and unsteady against her skin.

She moved her hand, and he caught it and pulled it away.

'No. I'm hanging by a thread as it is. Turn round.'

She turned, and he undid her bra and slid

the straps over her shoulders, his warm hands gliding down over her skin, sending goose bumps over it. She crossed her arms, suddenly acutely aware of the changes to her body since he'd last touched her like this.

What if it turns him off? What if he doesn't want me?

She felt the whisper of his breath, the touch of his lips on her shoulder, her neck, her ear, and she arched her neck to give him better access. His breath drifted like fire over her skin, and she could feel the slight graze of stubble, intoxicating as he laid a tiny line of kisses over her shoulder before turning her to face him.

Her arms were still crossed, but he lifted them gently away and cradled her breasts in safe, familiar hands.

'That's better,' he breathed, his thumbs stroking lightly over her nipples, and he feathered a kiss over her lips. 'You have no idea how much I've missed you,' he murmured against them, and she stifled a sob and lifted a hand to cradle his face.

'I've missed you, too. Missed this. The way you always knew how to touch me. Kiss me...'

His mouth found hers again, greedy now, and she slid her hands down his back and under his jeans, her fingers cupping taut, firm buttocks that tensed under her touch. He rocked against her, then pulled away, ditched the jeans and underwear in one hasty swipe and came back to her, the hard jut of his erection nudging hot and needy against the bowl of her pelvis.

And then he swore and stepped out of reach, his chest heaving.

'Stop. I could get you pregnant,' he muttered, and turned his head away. 'Dammit, we weren't doing this. If I'd known…'

She reached out and took his hands. 'I've got an IUCD,' she told him, suddenly glad that she hadn't had it removed.

He stared at her. 'Truly?'

'Yes, truly. I wouldn't lie to you about something like that.'

She felt the hiss of his outbreath as he pulled her back into his arms, toppling her onto the bed in a tangle of arms and legs. His mouth found hers, plundering it, their tongues duelling as her body arched against his. His hands were everywhere, driving her higher and higher until she was sobbing, and then he was there, filling her with one long, slow thrust, his breath shuddering against her shoulder as he dropped his head against hers and held her, motionless, for an endless moment.

And then he started to move, slowly at first and then building, building as her legs locked around him and his mouth found hers again, stifling her scream as he tipped her over the edge into ecstasy.

She felt him shudder, heard the ragged groan dragged from somewhere deep inside him, then the slackening of his muscles as he lay against her, his breath hot against her skin.

Her heart slowed as their breathing levelled, and he shifted so he could see her face.

'You're crying,' he said softly, and wiped the tears away with a gentle finger.

'I'd forgotten,' she said simply, and she closed her eyes and bent her head down, and he gathered her closer and cradled her as she cried for all they'd lost.

It was still lost, it always would be, and doing this was so foolish. It was only going to make it hurt more, because this was all they could ever have. A few stolen moments in the midst of their fractured lives.

If only Amelie were hers, if Billy and Phoebe were his—but they weren't, and never would be, and no amount of wishful thinking was going to change that.

Could they blend their families? Her two children, his two children? And then what about his mother? And then Kath and Steve on the fringes, adding to the complexity of their lives?

Would Elizabeth move out and go back to her flat and leave Emily in sole charge of both families? Where would Kath stay when she came? And Charlie?

And more importantly, what if, after all of that juggling and compromise, it still didn't work? What could they say to the children, those poor children who'd already lost so much to divorce? How could it possibly be fair to ask them to do it all over again?

It couldn't, and it was too great a risk.

She shifted, swiping the fresh tears from her cheeks with a determined hand.

'Are you OK?' he murmured, his voice soft and filled with concern.

She nodded. 'I'm being stupid. I was just wishing we could turn back the clock, or even just start again from here, but we can't. I know we can't. There's too much at stake for all of us, and we just can't risk it. If it goes wrong—'

'Why should it?'

'Why shouldn't it? It did before. You went and slept with Sue for no very good reason that I can see, and then Steve left me when I thought we were all good and making it work, but I wasn't enough for him, just like I wasn't enough for you. And it doesn't matter what you say,' she added, cutting him off when he tried to speak, 'because it's true. If I'd been enough for you, you wouldn't have slept with her, and we'd be in a completely different place, but as it is I can't trust you not to hurt me again, like you did before, like Steve did—I'm not going there again, Oliver. I can't do it.'

He gave a ragged sigh and wiped away her tears with a gentle hand. 'It wasn't that,' he said, his voice heavy and sincere. 'It wasn't that you weren't enough. You just weren't there, and I was lonely. Lonely, and maybe a bit angry with you for not coming with me, and it was a stupid, stupid mistake and I've regretted it ever since.'

'But you knew I couldn't go. You could have stayed. I know you said you couldn't, but you could, if I'd mattered enough to you. You didn't have to go, but your career path came first, just like it did with Kath. You say she won't compromise, but then neither will you. You just want it all your own way, and you probably would have been the same with me.'

'That isn't true. And anyway, we weren't at that point. It might not have lasted.'

'Well, we'll never know, will we, because you never gave us that chance.'

'I was going to. I was coming back to you, and I instantly regretted sleeping with her. It was a huge mistake and I hated myself, and when I found out she was pregnant, I was devastated. I only stayed with her for the baby, and I never loved her the way I loved you.'

She searched his eyes, looking for the truth but not sure she'd recognize it if she saw it. 'I didn't know you loved me. Why didn't you tell me? I thought you didn't care or you would have stayed.'

He shrugged. 'I don't know. Protecting myself? Maybe also not letting it get too serious, because we were going to be apart for a year and I didn't know what might happen between us in that time, but I always cared and I've never stopped regretting that I hurt you. I thought maybe when I came back—but then it was too late. And you didn't tell me, either. You left it nineteen years to tell me that. And if it helps, I've never loved anyone since the way I—' He broke off, then added, 'The way I loved you.'

His eyes were steady, and she wondered what he'd been going to say. Love, not loved? Maybe.

'I never have, either. I think it broke me. I loved Steve, I was happy enough with him, but it wasn't like it was with you. I've never found that again.'

Until now…

His eyes searched hers, and he reached out a tentative hand and cradled her cheek tenderly.

'Can we try again?' he asked. 'Not involving the kids, but just—maybe we could have this. Just sometimes, like an oasis, a precious retreat where we can be together. Maybe even get away for the weekend from time to time, if the others could have the children.'

She hesitated. Could they? Did she dare? Although what did she have to lose? She loved him anyway, and it was going nowhere, but maybe…

'That would be nice. That would be really nice—but you have to know it can't go anywhere. It's just this, you and me.'

He nodded slowly, his eyes steady, but the silence was broken by a quiet buzzing and he gave a frustrated sigh.

'I bet that's Kath.'

He rolled away from her and sat up, fishing in his jeans pocket for his phone, and then he swore softly and answered it.

He took the phone out onto the landing, and she lay in bed and listened to one side of what sounded like a rather fraught conversation about Amelie. His voice changed and she guessed he was speaking to his daughter, then it changed back again and she heard her name mentioned, and he came back into the bedroom and sat down on the edge of the bed and sighed.

She laid a hand on his arm. 'Trouble?' she murmured, and he turned to face her, his eyes too dark to read.

'Yeah. She won't go to sleep, she says her mother hates her, which she doesn't—she just doesn't have a clue how to be a mother. She also told Kath you were nicer.'

'Ouch. That's why you were talking about me. Is she jealous?'

'No, just protective, I think, although I don't know how she can justify that as she left me. Anyway, it's none of her business.'

'It is if I'm influencing her daughter. I can understand that. Do you want to go home?'

Did he?

'Honestly? Yes, but I'm not going to. I can't. They have to resolve this, and they have to find a way to be friends. But it is a nightmare, especially her unreliability. You don't know how lucky you are with Steve.'

She smiled wryly. 'I wouldn't say I was lucky, but he's a good father. It hasn't always been easy, though, and it's only because his wife is so accepting that it works at all.'

'Yeah. I haven't even met Kath's partner,

and Amelie has no idea what their life is like or where they live or anything.'

'Maybe you should take her over there to meet him?'

He shrugged. 'Maybe one day.' He put his phone on her bedside table and lay down facing her, before reaching out a hand and stroking her hair back off her face.

'You OK?' she asked, and he nodded.

'I guess so,' he said, but he wasn't, not really, because Kath's call had been a brutal reminder that the status quo was finely balanced and could all come crashing down at any time and their little oasis could be wiped out at a stroke.

And again, he was swamped as Emily had been by all the if-onlys.

If only they'd stayed together. If only she was Charlie and Amelie's mother—but they hadn't, and she wasn't, and nothing he could do would ever change that.

Her hand reached out and cradled his face, the tenderness in her touch nearly undoing him.

'Don't worry about her,' she murmured. 'She's not going to come to any harm, and you can talk to Kath tomorrow. For now, you need to sleep, and so do I. I have to be at work at seven.'

'You do. I'm sorry. Come here,' he murmured, opening his arms, and she moved into them with a quiet sigh.

'It'll be all right, Oliver. Don't worry.'

Easier said than done.

Emily drifted off to sleep, and he lay there, staring up at the ceiling and wondering how his daughter was coping with a mother who didn't know how to love her, and whether he could ever win Emily's trust again. What a mess...

He woke her with a kiss, which ended up with her running for a hasty shower and getting to work in the nick of time with a smile on her face, and by the time she got home he was gone.

She made her bed, lingering over the pillows, burying her nose in the scent of him. Could they do this? Make it work?

Maybe.

She heard Steve's car and ran down, and he kissed the children goodbye, and then after they'd run upstairs she had an interesting conversation with him about Oliver.

The children had clearly been talking about him, but she put him straight—or almost—about their relationship, although she wasn't sure he believed her.

He got in the car and drove away, leaving her thoughtful. He wanted to see her settled with someone else? So did she, if only there weren't so many potential pitfalls in their way.

Too much at stake, and wishful thinking wouldn't change that, but she was glad he was open to the idea of her having a relationship. She wondered how Oliver had got on with Kath. She didn't envy him.

And he was right. She was lucky with Steve. At least for all his failings he loved his children deeply, and they loved him.

She went back inside, rounded up the children and they headed back to Oliver's house, the children predictably talking non-stop about Steve's puppy.

'Will Berry be here?' Phoebe asked as they turned onto Oliver's drive, and she shook her head.

'No, darling. She's with Amelie's grandma. She's her dog, not theirs. You know that.'

'Why can't *we* have a dog?' Billy said, and she sighed.

'You know why. It's not fair. I'm working.'

'You could stop working,' Phoebe said, and she laughed.

'What would we eat? Where would we live?'

'We could live with Amelie,' her little daughter said innocently, and Emily felt her heart squeeze in her chest.

If only life were that easy…

She followed them in, and within seconds they were out in the garden with Amelie, playing in the den. Oliver was sitting on the bench, and he smiled and patted the seat beside him as she approached.

'You OK?' he asked, and she plonked herself down beside him with a tiny laugh.

'Oh, I'm fine. The kids want a puppy.'

'Seriously?'

'Very seriously. Steve's got one, Amelie's got one, why can't we have one?'

He chuckled. 'Yeah, they aren't great with logistics.'

'Oh, they are. They suggested I gave up work and we came and lived with you.'

His eyes met hers searchingly. 'And?'

She laughed again. 'Nice little fantasy. Just a few things in the way.'

He looked over to the children, running in and out of the den, gathering scattered toys, their excited chatter filling the air, and then back at her.

'We wouldn't have to pretend any more,' he said softly, and she looked away and swallowed.

'Oliver, we can't. You know we can't. Compartments, remember?'

'I remember. I also remember how good it felt to hold you last night.'

She felt his hand brush hers, his fingers tightening around her own, and she gave his a gentle squeeze and eased her hand away. 'We can't do this. They're getting in deep enough as it is. They don't need any added complications.'

'Is that what we are? A complication?'

She met his eyes. 'Well, aren't we? And talking of complications, how did it go with Kath?'

He sighed and looked away. 'OK, I suppose. I think they had fun. Amelie was just trying it on, but she does that.' He got to his feet. 'You stay here and keep an eye on them. I'll go and finish off in the kitchen.'

Keeping their new relationship in a separate compartment proved even harder than Oliver had expected, especially after that conversation, because playing in the back of his mind was always the image of the children in the garden with a new puppy, and him and Emily together.

Married?

No. That was never to happen, for a whole

bunch of sound reasons, but it didn't stop him fantasizing about it and wishing it could be.

And every day that passed made it more and more difficult to maintain his perspective, not because of anything Emily or the children said or did, but because every day at work she was just *there*, right under his nose, and every morning and evening she was in his house, in his space, in his sight, and those memories, those longings, were now well and truly refreshed.

Even if he couldn't see her, he could hear her voice, imagine what she was doing, and he wanted more. He wanted all of it, but it was a minefield because their lives were too complicated, and anyway, she'd made it clear as day that that was never going to happen.

Kath didn't help. They'd made some progress over the weekend, but not enough, and then two days before she was due back, she had to cancel because her Japanese client was flying in again and she couldn't reschedule him.

Amelie was gutted, and so was he, not only for Amelie but also because that was his time with Emily, a time they'd both been looking forward to, and it was snatched away from them.

He was at work, of course, just finishing

off some notes in Resus when her message landed like a lead balloon, and he could have screamed. He didn't, he just punched the wall and hurt his hand, and Emily found him rubbing his knuckles ruefully.

'What have you done?'

'I might have accidentally hit the wall.'

She studied his face, and he could see her mind working. She cocked her head on one side.

'She's bailed again, hasn't she?' she said, and he nodded.

'Yup.'

Her shoulders dropped. 'Oh, Oliver. What are you going to do?'

'I have no idea. She needs a mother, and Kath just doesn't seem able to step up to the plate. It's not that she doesn't want to. It's just that unless she makes some pretty drastic changes to her work–life balance, she can't do any more. She's basically incapable of saying no to a client.'

'But she can say no to her daughter.'

'Apparently so. I think it's pressure from her boss, but whatever, it's not helping. Anyway, what's going on? Anything in particular need my attention out there?'

'No, it's quiet, so we could go and get a coffee—or not,' she added, picking up the red phone. 'Yoxburgh Park ED.'

She scribbled down the information, hung up and put a call over the Tannoy.

'Code Red, adult trauma call, ten minutes. Code Red, adult trauma call, fifteen minutes.'

His eyebrows creased together. 'Two?'

'Yup. A car's gone through the barrier at the top of a slip road and fallen twenty feet into the field beyond. They've got the driver out, he's on the way, and they're just releasing the passenger.'

'Young men?'

'No. Looks like a married couple, apparently. The man's in the air ambulance, leg and chest injuries, query aorta, GCS twelve at scene, and the woman's coming by road. She has head injuries and query spinal injuries and GCS is seven, so it's not looking great. She wasn't wearing a seat belt, apparently.'

She put out a call to the most relevant departments, ordered extra units of O neg, and as the room started to fill they could hear the air ambulance coming in to land.

'Here we go again,' she murmured, and went out to meet them, leaving Oliver to prep the team.

By the time he'd been wheeled into Resus, the man had deteriorated significantly. An ultrasound showed damage to his aorta, so he was taken straight to Joe Baker and Matt Hunter in the Interventional Radiology Surgical suite, leaving them free to focus on the woman.

She was on a spinal board, but she had no reflexes, and by the time she'd arrived her pupils were unequal and she was fitting, and she had cerebro-spinal fluid leaking out of her ear.

'Right, we need an urgent CT to see what's going on in her head,' he said, and as soon as they'd stopped the fitting and were satisfied that she was stable, she was taken down to Imaging.

The results arrived back almost as she did, and they confirmed all his fears.

'OK, she's got a massive subdural haemorrhage and a basal skull fracture. This is very not good.' He flashed the penlight in her eyes, but both pupils had blown and were unreactive, and moments later her heart slowed to a halt.

He gave a heavy sigh and looked around at his colleagues.

'OK, I'm calling it. Are we all agreed?'

They all nodded, as he'd known they would. Her situation was hopeless and any further intervention would be futile and an insult to her dignity.

He looked up at the clock. 'Time of death—eleven fifty-six. Sorry, guys. Are you all OK?'

They nodded, but the mood was definitely sombre, and he let out a slow, heavy sigh. 'Are the relatives here?'

'I think their son might be in the family room, talking to the police,' a nurse told him, and he nodded.

'OK, I'll go and talk to him. Thank you, everyone.'

He turned and met Emily's eyes, and she smiled sadly at him. 'You OK to do this, or shall I?'

'No, I'll do it,' he murmured. 'I shouldn't be too long, and then we'll go and get that coffee if it's quiet.'

She was waiting for him when he emerged looking grim-faced, and by a miracle the department was all ticking over nicely, so they went out into the park and he turned his face up to the sun and heaved a sigh of relief.

'Oh, that's better.'

'How did you get on with the son?'

'Oh, he's in bits. His mother had just phoned him to say his father wanted a divorce, and he was still talking to her when they crashed. His father was yelling abuse at his mother, and he thinks he might have crashed deliberately because she screamed, "What are you doing?" an instant before the crash.'

'Oh, no! That's awful.'

'Yeah. He thinks his father was probably trying to kill them both. Was there any word on him?'

She shook her head. 'No, nothing so far, but he's a mess, too. I wouldn't be surprised if he loses his right leg, and that's if he survives the injury to his aorta.'

'Well, if he does, he could be facing a murder charge. The son's told the police everything he knows. It makes me grateful that Kath's just a pain and not a psychopath.'

They grabbed sandwiches and coffees and headed out, but the café was busy so they sat on the grass under a tree and ate and drank in silence, their thoughts still on the couple.

'Are you all right?' he asked her after a moment, and she nodded.

'I guess. It's just so horrible for the family. How's your mother, talking of families?'

'Oh, she's making progress. Her left wrist is OK, so she can do much more for herself. She's talking about coming home at the weekend, so I've said I'll pick her up on Saturday morning.'

'Well, that's good, isn't it?'

He looked across at her, and she could see concern in his eyes. 'I don't know. She'll try and do stuff to help out. I know she will. I'll have to read her the riot act and she'll give me that look and do it anyway.'

She laughed. 'Don't worry, Oliver, I can be firm with her.'

'Only when you're there, and you're working this weekend and Kath's not there, so I'll have to dress and undress her.'

'Unless I stay over?'

He sighed. 'Could you? That would be really kind of you.'

'Well, I'm not going to be doing anything else on Friday and Saturday night, am I?' she said wryly, and he groaned and shook his head.

'Don't. It was our time, this weekend.'

'I know, but there'll be others.'

'I hope so. I'm so mad with Kath for bailing.'

'Maybe there's something else going on. Why is she so driven? Has she ever been poor?'

He snorted and turned his attention back to his coffee, taking a moment before he spoke. 'No. Her family are wealthy, they're all high achievers, her father was a hedge fund manager and her brother is someone high up in one of the big investment banks. They have money running through their veins.'

'So maybe she feels pressured to equal their success?'

He looked at her thoughtfully. 'Maybe—but if her own daughter isn't enough to make her change, then I don't know what is.'

'Maybe you've made it too easy.'

He laughed. 'You wouldn't say that if you'd seen me two weeks ago. I didn't make it easy, believe me.'

He pulled out his phone, glanced at it and got to his feet, pulling her up. 'Time to go back.'

They walked in just as his phone pinged, and he pulled it out and read the message, then looked at her and she knew it was bad news.

'The driver?'

He nodded and gave a heavy sigh. 'And we think we've got problems? That poor family. I'd better go and tell the team.'

To her surprise, when she and the children got back after the school run on Friday, they were greeted by Berry.

The poor dog was nearly beside herself with excitement, tearing round in circles from one child to another, so Emily opened the door and sent them all out into the garden, then tapped on the dividing door and went in to see Elizabeth.

She was sitting in her chair by the window,

watching the children, and she turned towards her with a big smile.

'Hello, Emily!'

'Hello, you!' she said, giving her a hug and a kiss. 'I wasn't expecting you to be here. I thought Oliver was picking you up tomorrow morning?'

'He was, but a friend offered to drop me home.'

'Oh, that's kind. So how are you doing? Are you OK?'

'I'm fine, thank you. So much better. Very bored with it all, and the sling's really annoying, but I'll do and at least it doesn't hurt now, and it's lovely to be home.' She reached out and took Emily's hand with her left one, and gave it a squeeze. 'Oliver says you've been an absolute star. I'm so grateful to you for looking after them for me.'

'You don't need to be. It's been a pleasure and the least I could do,' she said, returning the squeeze, 'and I think the children have quite enjoyed it.'

Elizabeth looked out of the window, a fond smile on her face. 'They do seem to get on very well,' she said, and Emily wasn't sure but she had a sneaky feeling it was a loaded comment. Was Elizabeth matchmaking?

No, surely not...

'Yes, they do, most of the time, which is lucky,' she said, and changed the subject. 'So, Oliver thinks you're going to be really silly and try and do too much before you've had time to heal properly, but I've told him I know you're not that foolish and there's nothing very much you'll need to do during the day, so I'm sure you'll be fine while I'm not here, won't you?'

Elizabeth turned and looked up at her from her chair, a little smile tugging at her mouth.

'What *are* you suggesting, Emily?'

'Nothing at all, because I know you won't do anything rash,' she said innocently.

They exchanged smiles, and Elizabeth shook her head and chuckled. 'You're a dear girl. Such a pity about you and Oliver.' Her smile faded as she looked out of the window at the children, and she sighed. 'I gather Kath's not coming this weekend, letting the child down yet again. She couldn't be less like you. It's such a shame. I don't understand her at all.'

Definitely matchmaking...

'I'm sure she has her reasons,' she said calmly, refusing to be drawn into that minefield. 'I have to take the children over to Steve soon. He normally picks them up but he can't today, so I said I'd do it, but is there anything I can do for you before I go?'

'What are you going to do with Amelie?'

'I was going to take her with me. Why?'

'Because I'm here, and I'm not doing anything. You won't be long, will you?'

'Half an hour, maybe a bit more?'

'Well, leave her here with me. I'm sure we can manage. I'm not that incapacitated.'

She smiled. 'No, you're not, and I'm sure she'll love that. She's missed you. If you don't mind, that would be lovely. I'll get you some tea before I go.'

CHAPTER EIGHT

SHE WAS BACK from Steve's not long after five, and she found Amelie sitting with her grandmother reading, the dog curled up against her side.

'You three look cosy,' she said with a smile. 'Is it nice having Grandma and Berry back?'

'Really, *really* nice,' she said, and she bounced up and ran over to hug Emily. 'What's for supper? Can I help you in the kitchen?' she asked, and Emily looked down at her and wondered how anything could possibly be more important to her mother than this little girl and her happiness.

Not your business...

She smiled at her. 'Yes, of course you can help me, sweetheart. What would you like for supper? There's some of that pasta bake left from yesterday, or we can make something else. What did you have for lunch?'

'Jacket potato and cheese and beans,' she

said, tugging the fridge door open. 'So what can I have?'

Something healthy, but what? She peered over Amelie's shoulder into the fridge. 'How about a Thai fish and vegetable curry, like I did before? You liked that, and Grandma will be able to eat it with one hand, so Daddy and Grandma and I can have it later.'

'Can I stay up and eat with you?'

Could she? Oliver was pretty strict about bedtimes, but the child's mother had bailed on her, and anyway, it was the weekend. She smiled. 'You know what? I think that would be lovely. You don't have to get up early tomorrow, and it's a bit of a celebration because Grandma's back, so why not? Just this once.'

By the time he got home just after seven, he was utterly ravenous and completely exhausted. He hadn't stopped all day, and James had sent him home after his last patient in Resus.

'We can finish off. You go,' he'd said, and Oliver had opened his mouth to argue, shut it and left before he got involved in another case.

And now he was home, to find his mother in the sitting room and Berry overjoyed to see him again.

He cuddled the dog first, because she was the most demanding, then hugged his mother.

'So how come you're here?' he asked, puzzled. 'I was picking you up tomorrow.'

'Douglas gave me a lift.'

He stared at her, puzzled. 'Douglas? Douglas *Buchanon*?'

His father's old friend? Surely not…

She met his eyes briefly and then looked away. 'I told him about my hand, so he popped over to see me.'

Popped? 'I didn't realize he lived anywhere near here.'

'Oh, yes, he moved to Aldeburgh about seven or eight years ago, just before Joanna died, and we've always kept in touch. He took me out to lunch a few times after I bought my flat, but obviously I've hardly seen him for the last eighteen months. Anyway, I think he just wanted to make sure my hand had been done properly, but it turns out he knows the surgeon who did my op and he rates him, so he was happy. Anyway, when I said I was coming back here this weekend, he offered me a lift and I thought it would save you a journey, so I said yes.'

'That was kind of him. I'm glad you're still in touch.'

'Yes, so am I,' she said, and he thought she coloured slightly.

Surely not? His mum and Douglas? And how much had they been seeing of each other before she'd come to his rescue in London? Maybe more than she was saying.

'Where's Amelie?' he asked to change the subject, even though he could hear them in the kitchen.

'Cooking supper with Emily.'

'Good, I'm starving. I'll go and chivvy them.' He headed to the kitchen, and Amelie ran over and threw herself at him, brimming with excitement.

'Daddy, Daddy, I'm making curry with Emily, and guess what? I'm staying up and eating with you and Grandma!'

'Are you, indeed?' he asked, scooping her up, and met Emily's slightly guilty eyes. 'And whose idea was that?'

'Mine,' Amelie said, 'but Emily said it would be OK just this once because it's the weekend and I don't have to get up in the morning. Plus Grandma's come home, so it's a celebration.'

His lips twitched, and so did Emily's, and he had to look away before he laughed.

'Well, that's all right then,' he said, and kissed Amelie and put her down, then looked at Emily again. 'How long will it take? Do I have time to shower?'

'Ten minutes? I just need to put the fish in and cook the rice.'

'Brilliant. Make plenty. I haven't eaten all day and I'm absolutely starving. Amelie, why don't you lay the table while she does that?'

While he put his daughter to bed after supper, Emily unpacked Elizabeth's bag and helped her get ready for bed, and by the time she'd done that and put the kettle on, Oliver was down again.

'Where's Mum?' he asked.

'In bed reading. She needed the sling off. Want a drink?'

'Yeah, but not coffee. I've been mainlining it all day. A nice cold beer would slip down a treat.'

She smiled at him. 'Yes, I thought it might. You were up to your eyes every time I walked past Resus. Long day?'

He laughed a little hysterically and walked out. 'Give me two minutes. I'm just going to say goodnight to my mother,' he threw over his shoulder, still grinning, and she smiled and made herself a cup of fruit tea. By the time he came back, she was on the sofa with her tea, his beer on the table beaded with moisture, and he dropped onto the sofa beside her, picked up the glass and downed half of it.

'Oh, my word, that's better,' he said, putting his feet up and rolling his head towards her, a smile teasing his lips. 'Thanks for sorting Mum out. She says you laid the law down about overdoing it.'

Her lips twitched. 'Good. I'm glad she realized.'

'Oh, she realized. I think a few people have been pretty firm with her, too, so hopefully she'll behave.'

'Do you know why she came home today? I thought you were picking her up tomorrow, but she said a friend brought her home.'

His brow creased a little. 'Yeah, and that's quite interesting. He's an old colleague of my father's, a family friend. He was widowed a year or two before my father died, and they've kept in touch. He was a hand surgeon, oddly, so she told him about her hand, and apparently he doesn't live far away, so he's been to visit her, and he offered her a lift, but...'

'But what? That all sounds perfectly reasonable.'

He laughed. 'I don't know. I just got a funny feeling there was more to it than that, and she was avoiding my eye a bit.'

'Really? Do you think it's significant?'

'I don't know what to think. She said that after she bought her flat up here he took her out for lunch a few times, so maybe. I mean, for goodness' sake, she's entitled to a life, and to her privacy, but—I don't know. It's probably all totally innocent. I'm just a bit surprised.'

She searched his eyes. 'Would you mind if they were more than just friends?' she asked carefully, and he shrugged.

'It's not really up to me, is it? I know Dad wouldn't want her to be unhappy and lonely, and she's been pretty sad for quite a while, but... I don't know... It would just be really weird. Would I mind? No, I don't think so, and if she wants to be with someone, she couldn't have chosen a nicer, more decent person. To be honest, I don't know what to think. I just hope one of them isn't reading more into it than is meant.'

'Is that likely?'

'No idea. No doubt time will tell, but she seems happier than she's been in a while. Anyway, enough about her, how was your day?'

'Not as busy as yours, thank goodness. Want to debrief?'

His laugh morphed into a groan, and he shook his head. 'No, I'm fine. It was just relentless. Every time I thought I might get a second to grab something to eat or drink, there was another one, then another—James took over and sent me home in the end.'

'Did you argue with him?'

He gave a rueful chuckle. 'No, I was beyond arguing and I was so hungry I was about to eat my own arm. That curry was delicious, by the way. Thank you. And thank you for letting Amelie stay up. She loved it.'

She pulled a face. 'I wasn't sure you'd approve, but—her weekend's gone AWOL, and—you know.'

'Yeah, I know.' He turned his head and met her eyes. 'So's ours,' he said softly.

His hand found hers, and he tugged her closer, wrapping his arm around her and resting his head against hers with a quiet sigh. 'I thought by now we'd be tucked up in bed together, but it's not going to happen this weekend.'

'No,' she said, feeling a twinge of sadness. 'Still, we get this time together every night after the children are in bed.'

'Yup. I'm not sure if that's a good thing,' he said with a wry smile. 'The frustration's killing me.'

She reached up and cradled his jaw in her hand, and he turned his head and touched his lips to hers.

Not for long, because it just made the longing worse, and then he pulled away a fraction, resting his forehead against hers with a sigh.

'I wish Kath had come this weekend,' he mumbled.

'I know, but there'll be other times. It's just disappointing.'

He moved away, slumping back against the sofa with a frustrated sigh. 'Tell me about it. And if we're feeling like this, how is Amelie feeling?'

'She'll be fine. It's half-term in a week, and she'll be busy with holiday club for some of it, and then Kath's coming over on Thursday for the weekend.'

'But I'm working then, and so are you.'

'Not at night, and this won't last for ever,' she murmured. 'Your mother will be able to do more soon, so I can move home, and we'll get those weekends back.'

'Will we? Suddenly that doesn't feel like enough, and anyway, Charlie will be here, so I'll have to explain to him that I want to spend the nights with you, and that is *not* a conversation I want to have with my seventeen-year-old son.'

She winced. 'No, I can see why. We could spend the evenings together—couldn't we?' she suggested.

He rolled his head towards her, his eyes

filled with frustration and a longing that made her heart tug.

'We could, but I want more than that, Em— so much more. An evening doesn't feel like nearly enough,' he said.

It didn't, but deep inside her was still that fear that it could all go wrong. It had before. Could she trust him now? Could she trust herself?

'It has to be enough, and anyway, it's not for long. Charlie won't be here for ever and then maybe...' she said, and kissed his cheek before moving away, because being so close to him was nothing short of torture. So near and yet so far...

'I think I might go to bed. I've got work in the morning and I'm tired,' she said, and he nodded.

'You do that. I'm going to ring Charlie, tell him Grandma's home. I'll see you tomorrow. Sleep well.'

He sat for a while without moving, staring at nothing, wondering where this could possibly lead them.

If anywhere. Could they make a go of it? The children seemed to get on well enough, and she'd slotted seamlessly back into his life and made him feel whole again for the first time in decades.

Yet still in the back of his mind there was that lingering doubt, the risk to the children's happiness if it all went wrong—it had before, for both of them, with two of their three marriages failing due to work pressure.

And being a consultant hadn't really changed that for him. He still had to work some weekends, some nights, and without his mother's help he would have been sunk.

So what if his mother and Douglas got married and she moved out? Where on earth would that leave him?

If it was what they wanted, he wouldn't— couldn't—contemplate standing in their way, but what if he already was? What if they'd been much more in touch than she'd let on, and they wanted to be together, but because of his situation his mother felt duty bound to stay with him and Amelie?

Of course, if he and Emily were together it wouldn't be a problem, but they weren't, and it certainly wasn't a good enough reason to escalate their relationship when neither of them were ready for it.

But if he wasn't with Em and things did get serious between his mother and Douglas, then the impact on his life would be huge.

Back to the au pair idea? A live-in house-keeper? Or go part-time and sacrifice his career?

He dropped his head back and growled with frustration. How could it *get* any more complicated?

Emily left work late on Sunday afternoon, and she found a message on her phone that made her chuckle.

Gone to the beach. Back when we've built the biggest sandcastle in the world—will take photos!

It was followed by a few photos of Amelie looking immensely proud in front of her sand-castle, and a lovely selfie of Oliver with his arm round his daughter. Lucky them. She felt a pang of envy, but it was pointless. She had to work to pay her mortgage, she knew that, but the weekends were always her least favourite shifts. Not that she had anything else to do while the children were with Steve.

Oliver's car still wasn't there when she turned onto the drive, and as she went into the hall, she could hear Elizabeth's phone ringing through the slightly open door to her annexe. She heard her say, 'Hello,' followed by a startled exclamation. 'Oh, no! Hang on—oh, I can't reach...'

Emily dumped her bag on the floor and tapped on the door. 'Elizabeth, are you all right? Anything I can do?'

'Oh, Emily, bless you,' she said, looking a bit flustered. 'I've dropped my phone under the chair and I can't get to it with this stupid, stupid arm and Oliver's not here.'

'Of course—don't move. I can reach it.'

She pulled it out, and she could hear a man's voice asking if she was still there.

'Here you go,' she said, handing it back with a smile.

'Thank you. Douglas, I'm so sorry. It's this stupid arm,' she was saying as Emily went out. She closed the annexe door behind her, but not before she heard a light-hearted laugh.

Was Oliver right? She had a feeling he might be.

And if he was, and if they got together, then where would that leave him and Amelie? She was almost certain Douglas wouldn't be happy living here in the little annexe that was Elizabeth's home, and if she wasn't here, how would Oliver cope?

What if he couldn't find a suitable replacement, someone to live in and look after them both as his mother had been doing until her accident? She was so lucky to have Steve nearby, but Oliver didn't have that luxury, with Kath in another country.

Being a single parent was a nightmare of juggling and compromise, but no matter how accommodating the other ED staff were, they had to have appropriate levels of staffing and James was struggling to provide twenty-four-seven consultant cover as it was. He often ended up doing more than his fair share, so how could Oliver cut his hours?

Unless she stayed?

No. That wasn't an option, not unless they were properly together, and there was no way she was ready for that yet, and probably not ever. She still wasn't sure she could trust him with her heart, and anyway, she was still scarred from her divorce, and so were the children, and she didn't think Oliver was ready, either—and even if he was, it certainly wasn't a good enough reason for them to take that step.

Unless she helped him on an ad hoc basis, having Amelie when he worked nights—and she was totally jumping the gun.

There was no suggestion whatsoever that Elizabeth was going to marry Douglas! Sheer speculation, and probably utterly unfounded.

And then she heard another laugh through

the door, and thought maybe it wasn't unfounded. And that could have serious impli-
cations for them all.

They were almost home from the beach when
a strange car pulled up on the drive. He saw
Emily's children waving through the windows,
and the driver got out and opened the back
doors.

He walked towards him. 'You must be
Steve,' he said, brushing the sand off his hand
and extending his arm with a smile, and as
they shook hands he met a pair of searching
eyes and got the distinct feeling he was being
interviewed. 'I'm—'

'Oliver!' Phoebe shrieked, getting out of the
car, and she flung her arms around his legs and
hugged him, and he looked down and smiled
at her.

'Hi, Phoebe,' he said, ruffling her hair gently. 'Had a good time?'

'Yup. Daddy wants to meet Berry. Come
on, Amelie, let's go and get her,' she said, the
two girls running for the door.

He felt his mouth twitch, and met Steve's
eyes again, not at all convinced it was the dog
he wanted to meet. 'I think you'd better come
in.'

Billy had already run inside, and he came

tumbling out with Berry, who was so pleased to see the children that she hardly paid Steve any attention at all.

'Come on, you lot, inside,' he said, chivvying them all back in, then he turned back to Steve as they went through the door. 'Can I get you a drink?'

It was after nine before they got a chance to sit down, and she flopped onto her end of the sofa and put her feet on his lap.

'Oh, that's better. Steve likes you, by the way,' she added, and he turned and looked at her.

'A man of excellent taste,' he said with a lazy grin. 'I liked him, too. He's a nice guy.'

'He is. It's just a pity he didn't realize what his priorities were before he met me.'

Oliver rolled his eyes. 'Yeah, we've both got one of those. Come here, you need a cuddle.'

'I do, or you do?' she asked, trying not to smile, and he leaned over and reached for her.

'I do,' he said, his smile gentle and teasing and oh-so sexy...

She went into his arms without argument, settling down with her head on his shoulder and wishing life wasn't so ridiculously complicated. 'So how's your weekend been?'

He laughed softly. 'Better than yours, I imagine.'

'Oh, don't. It was a madhouse and I'm only grateful I'm not doing nights. Still, just this week to go and I get five days off, and then the following weekend we can be together again.' Unless... 'What will you do if Kath doesn't come?'

He shook his head. 'She has to come, and if she doesn't Amelie's already booked in for holiday club, so she could just spend the whole week there.'

'Or she can come to me midweek and you can keep holiday club in reserve for the weekend?'

He shook his head. 'No. She has to be here, and anyway, you do too much for us already. You need time with your kids on your own, Emily. They can't get too used to this. I know it's short-term, but they're all getting closer, and...'

They were. She nodded slowly. 'I know. I agree,' she told him. 'And actually, I think your mother can manage to dress and undress herself just about now, and she even managed a shower this morning with her arm in a bag, so if you're OK with it, I was thinking I could take the children to my parents for the weekend, because we haven't seen them for ages.'

He turned his face towards her and dropped a kiss on her hair. 'Good idea,' he murmured, but she could tell that, like her, none of this was what he really wanted.

But what they wanted wasn't necessarily what they could have, and at least they both realized that. Not that it made it any easier...

'That was a bit close to home.'

Emily looked up and searched his eyes as they walked out of Resus on Friday. He'd come in to join her in a futile attempt to save the life of a patient who'd suffered a massive heart attack, and his widow was in there now, saying a heartbroken goodbye to the man she'd loved for very many years, stricken with grief and shocked to the core because he had no history of any previous heart problems. Just like Oliver's father...

'I'm sure it was. Are you OK?'

'Yeah, I'm fine. It is what it is and we can't save them all. I've spoken to Kath, by the way. She's coming with Hans and they want to stay in a hotel.'

She stared at him in astonishment. 'Well, how does that work?'

'It doesn't, for us. They'll have to get up early so they're at mine by six, and stay with her till I'm home, but that'll only cover my working hours. I'll talk to her, see if I can change her mind, but she said she had something important to tell me, and she sounded— I don't know. Different. Happier, maybe, so I don't know what that's about.'

'Do you think they're getting married?'

'I have no idea, but if she won't bend that means yet again we lose our weekend nights together, and then Charlie comes. It's going to be ages before we get another chance and the frustration is killing me.'

He looked up at the board to see who was waiting, but it was looking reasonable. 'Coffee while the going's good?' he suggested, and then they heard the red phone ring and he rolled his eyes.

'Oh, now, why did you say that?' she murmured, and as the person who'd answered the phone put a call out on the Tannoy, she went back into Resus with Oliver.

A nurse was leading the sobbing woman out to the family room to make her a drink while her husband's body was moved, and Oliver watched them go, his face drawn.

'Can you handle this next case? I might go and talk to her.'

'Do you need to?'

'Yes, because I understand,' he said quietly. 'Unless you need me?'

She shook her head. 'No, I'll be fine. You do that. I can always call someone else. Just—be kind to yourself.'

His smile wrenched at her heart, but she let him go and made herself focus on the next patient, but at the back of her mind was the perennial threat to their time alone together.

How on earth could they make this work? Because from where she was standing, it didn't look like they could.

By the time he got home, Emily was ready to leave. Their stuff was packed in the car, and she'd remade the beds in case Kath had a change of heart.

'Everything OK?' she asked, and he nodded.

'Ish. Can we have a word while the children are outside?'

'Sure. What's up? Has she backed out again?'

'No, she won't back down about Hans coming and they won't stay here, even though I've offered. They'll be here every morning at six and they won't leave until I'm home, but— well, you know what it means. I'm so sorry.'

She closed her eyes and turned away, swallowing her disappointment.

'So that's that, then. You'll be here, not at mine.'

'You could be here, too.'

'No. Not with your mother here, not with Amelie here. We can't. You know that. It has to be at mine or not at all, and it's looking like not at all.'

She turned to face him, and his eyes were filled with an emotion she didn't want to analyse.

'I'm so sorry.'

'Don't be. I was half expecting it.'

'There'll be other times.'

'Maybe,' she said, not sure she could see how, and went out into the garden to call the children in.

'Do we have to go to Grandma and Grandad?' Billy asked. 'It's such a long way.'

'I know, but they're expecting us and it'll be lovely to see them. Come on. Say goodbye to Amelie and let's go.'

She met Oliver's eyes, and after a moment he looked away.

'Have a good time,' he said to the children, and then looked back at her and mouthed, 'I'm sorry.'

So was she, but there wasn't a thing either of them could do about it.

Kath and Hans arrived promptly at six on Thursday morning, just as he'd put some coffee on, and while it brewed they talked for a few minutes, which gave Kath just enough time to drop a couple of bombshells on him before they heard the sound of running feet.

'Daddy? Daddy, what time's Mummy coming...? Mummy!'

She threw herself at her mother, and Kath stooped down and hugged her hard, tears in her eyes.

'Hello, darling. Oh, I've missed you. Goodness, you've grown!'

Oliver turned away, glad they'd got to this point, sad that it had taken so long to reach it, but at least they were there now, and that, and Amelie, were all that mattered.

So he couldn't stay with Emily this weekend. Tough—and it was tough, but it was the least of his worries and this was hugely important news.

'So, who wants breakfast?' he asked.

'Me, me, me!' Amelie squealed, and he laughed and hugged her.

'Apart from you,' he said, and reached for the coffee.

Maybe it wouldn't be so bad after all...

CHAPTER NINE

IT WAS LATE on Thursday morning before she saw him again after her days off.

She'd arrived to find the department in uproar, and it was gone eleven before she'd dealt with the backlog in the cubicles.

She went to look for Oliver, and found him hunched over a computer in Resus.

She walked over to him with a smile. 'Hello, stranger. How's it going?'

He looked up from the computer and gave her a rueful smile. 'Hi. Sorry, really busy morning. I haven't had a second to call you. You OK?'

'Yes, fine. I've been really busy, too, but it's all suspiciously under control now, though, so I'm sort of waiting for the other shoe to drop.'

'Half-term. They're all on the beach having fun by now.'

'So they'll all be in with sunburn later. Fabulous.'

'Indeed. Look, I'm just finishing up these notes, and then I'm heading for a coffee. Got time to join me? I've got lots to tell you.'

'Absolutely! We might as well make the best of it while the going's good.'

'Tell me about it. Right, I'm done. Let's get out of here.' He pressed Save and they headed briskly for the café.

'So, spill the beans. Did Kath and Hans turn up on time? What's he like?' she asked him as they walked, and he laughed softly.

'I don't know. First impressions are good, but it's early days. He doesn't have children and he said he's always wanted them.'

She frowned. 'I hope that isn't the attraction.'

Oliver shook his head. 'I don't think it is. He told me he and his wife were never blessed with them—his words—and she died, and he's been alone ever since. He seems a very gentle person. He was lovely with Amelie, not at all pushy, and he didn't talk down to her, which I liked. Which is just as well, as he's going to be her stepfather. They're getting married.'

'Wow. OK. Did you know that?'

'Nope. And—wait for this—she's resigned.'

'To what?'

'Not to—from. Her job.'

She felt her eyes widen. 'Really? That's the last thing I expected!'

'Me, too. I was stunned. I don't know if it was because of what I said last time, or if it's been brewing a while, but she just lost it with them, by the sound of it. Anyway, she wants to see more of her daughter, and Amelie is over the moon.'

Emily felt her eyes fill with tears. 'Oh, that's lovely for her. For all of them, really. You must be so relieved.'

'I am. I can't tell you how much,' he said, and stopped at the counter. 'Right, what are you having?'

They picked up a sandwich to share, ordered their coffees and headed out into the park again. The benches were all full, but they found a free bistro table and sat down, his knees nudging hers, and he met her eyes, a sad smile playing round his lips.

'I'm sorry about our plans being trashed again,' he said softly. 'I'm really glad Kath's here and she's happy at last, but I just wish...'

She tried to smile back, but it was pointless. 'Me, too, but it is what it is and it's not for ever.'

'Thankfully not. So how are you doing?'

'Oh, OK, I suppose. It's always a bit flat without the children, but at least they're only ten miles away having fun with their step-brothers, unlike Charlie. I know he's coming over now, but most of the time he's in America, and I don't know how either of you cope with that.'

That sad smile again. 'Not well, to be honest, and I can't wait to hug him again. It's been so long, literally a year since we spent any appreciable length of time together, and I miss him so much.'

'So what will you do with him while he's here?'

'As much as I can. I've taken a lot of time off, but I need holiday time for Amelie and I can't afford to use it all and he's here three weeks. I can't do that.'

She laughed softly. 'Yes, I know how that goes. It's a constant juggling act when you're a single parent.'

'Well, hopefully it'll be better now with Kath doing a bit more of the heavy lifting, but we'll see how that goes, too. And for some of the time he's going to have to amuse himself, but that's fine. He says he wants to take a look at Cambridge, and he's thinking of applying for medicine there.'

She felt her eyes widen. 'He's going into medicine? Is he a masochist?'

He laughed. 'I know, I know. I've tried to

talk him out of it, but I'm a doctor, my father was a doctor, so was his father—as my grandmother would have said, it runs in the blood.'

That made her laugh, but it was a laugh tinged with sadness, because it was another three weeks where she'd hardly see him, and it was beginning to dawn on her just how deeply she was getting into this.

Not that she begrudged him that time with his son, it must be so precious, but it was becoming clearer by the day that their relationship as it was was unsustainable, and she couldn't see a way round it to save her life.

Two days in, and this was killing him.

Seeing Emily every day at work just ramped up the frustration, and if Kath had been at his, they could have been together every night. Just one evening would have been good, but they couldn't even do that, because his mother had decided to keep out of their way and had gone back to Catherine's until Sunday, so she couldn't babysit.

He drove home, went in and found Kath and Hans in the sitting room, with Amelie snuggled up between them in pyjamas and reading them a story.

She broke off, looked up and said, 'Daddy, sit down. I'm reading a story to you all.'

So he sat, and he listened as she stumbled through it with a tiny bit of prompting from Hans, and then she said, 'The end!' and shut the book, ran over to him and climbed onto his lap. 'Did you have a good day?' she asked, giving him a toothpasty kiss, and he smiled and hugged her.

'Yes, thank you. I had a very good day,' he lied. 'How was your day?'

'Brilliant! We went to a museum and saw all sorts of things, like dinosaur teeth and some bones, and when I grow up, I want to be a arkelol...'

'Archaeologist?' he offered, trying to keep a straight face, and she beamed.

'Yes! An arkelologist, and then I can dig up dinosaur bones and all sorts of stuff from gazillions of years ago!'

His face cracked into a smile, and he hugged her again, happy that she was happy, and that for now was enough. 'That sounds like a great thing to do. Right, I think it's probably bedtime now. Who do you want to put you to bed?'

'Mummy,' she said promptly, and wriggled off his lap and ran back to her, pulling her to her feet. 'Come on. You can read me another story.'

It was half an hour before Kath came down, and he spent it in the kitchen propped up against the worktop, getting to know—and like—the man who was going to be a key part of Amelie's life.

Then Kath walked in, and Oliver saw the warmth light their eyes as they smiled at each other, and he felt a pang of envy that they had that freedom. Unless...

'Amelie would like you to say goodnight,' she told him, and he nodded.

'OK.' He hesitated, then said, 'I don't suppose you'd be able to babysit tomorrow night, would you? Just for a few hours after I finish work?'

Kath's face fell. 'Oh, Oliver, I'm sorry, we can't. We've booked tickets for a late show at the theatre. We aren't busy tonight, though, but I don't suppose that's any good, is it?'

Would Emily be doing anything? He didn't think so. She'd probably be in the bath, if he knew her, or curled up on the sofa reading a book.

'It could be. Have you eaten? There's stuff in the fridge if not, or you could order a takeaway? I'll happily pay for it—'

'Don't be ridiculous.'

'Right, give me five minutes to check and to say goodnight to Amelie, and I'll let you know.'

He went upstairs, messaging Emily as he

went, and by the time he reached Amelie's door his phone had pinged.

In the bath. Come on over, I'll get out now. Have you eaten?

No.

OK. I'll get you something.

Yes! He punched the air, his face split by a smile of joy and relief, and went to say good-night to his daughter.

By the time he arrived, the door was on the latch and she was in the kitchen in a silky robe, stirring something on the hob. He toed off his shoes and walked up behind her, slid his arms round her waist and buried his face in the side of her neck with a contented sigh.

'Hello, you,' he mumbled, and she turned in his arms, looked up at him and smiled.

'Hello, you.'

He lowered his head and kissed her smile. 'You smell amazing,' he murmured, and then looked over her shoulder. 'What are you cooking?'

'Beans on toast. I don't really have anything else. Sorry.'

'Don't worry, that'll be fine. Anything I can do?'

'Pour us a glass of wine and talk to me,' she instructed, and he opened the bottle and told her about Amelie wanting to be an archaeologist.

'Well, this week, anyway. Last week she wanted to be a vet, and before that she was going to be an astronaut.'

'Coming down to earth, then, bit by bit,' she said with a grin, and he laughed. She slathered butter on his toast, poured the beans over and picked up the plate. 'Bring my wine,' she said, and headed for the dining table, and he followed her, still smiling.

'So, how long have we got?' she asked as he ate, and he shrugged.

'I said I'd be back by eleven. It's not long enough, but it's better than nothing and I just wanted to see you.' He scraped up the last mouthful, pushed his plate away and met her smiling eyes.

'We'd better not waste it, then,' she said softly, pulling him to his feet, and he followed her up to her room, his heart pounding.

She turned to face him, and he bent his head and kissed her while his hands found the tie on her robe and tugged it free. She was naked underneath, and he slid his hands inside, her skin warm under his fingers, nipples pebbling against his palms as he cradled her breasts, and he sighed into her mouth.

'Oh, you feel so good,' he mumbled, and moved on, laying kisses down over her throat, pausing over the beating pulse, then on down, over her collarbone, the slope of her right breast, the tautness of the nipple firm against his lips as he closed them round it and suckled deeply.

She moaned and arched against him, and he straightened, sliding the gown over her shoulders and staring down at her body, tracing it with a quivering fingertip.

She sucked in a shaky breath, and his control splintered.

Taking a step back he ripped off his T-shirt, shucking his jeans and underwear, kicking off his shoes as they fell into bed.

There was no need for foreplay, no time for finesse, no time for anything until he was buried inside her, her warmth around him, her body soft and yet firm against his, and then he slowed.

His mouth found hers again, tenderly now, sipping, searching, their bodies in tune as he slowly upped the pace, taking her with him every step of the way.

And when it was over, when their hearts had

slowed and their bodies cooled, he lay and held her in his arms and treasured every fleeting moment until he had to leave her...

They both worked on Saturday, but he wasn't there on Sunday because Kath and Hans were leaving, and it felt odd without him. She worked until four, went home and packed up their stuff, ready to go back to Oliver's for the coming week, but her heart was heavy.

Just five more nights, then Charlie would arrive, and she and the children would be back here at home for three weeks, and because Oliver would be off for much of it, she'd hardly see him.

And that mattered more than it should have done. More than she should have let it. He was getting under her skin, filling her thoughts, her mind, her heart—and her body ached for him. So much for compartments.

She put it out of her mind, loaded the car and drove to Oliver's house. Steve was taking the children straight there, and of course after they'd arrived and rushed in to see Amelie and Berry, Billy wanted something from their house.

'I need the chess set. Daddy's been teaching me to play chess, and I want to practise.'

'Oh, darling, you should have told me. I would have brought it. I'll get it tomorrow.'

'I've got a chess set,' Oliver volunteered, and Billy's eyes lit up.

'Really? Do you know how to play?'

'Yes. Well, I used to. I haven't played for ages.'

'Cool. I might beat you.'

To his credit Oliver kept a straight face, and nodded. 'You might,' he said, and met her eyes. 'Do you need a hand unloading the car?'

'That would be great. Why don't you all go in the garden with Berry while we do that?' she suggested, and the children ran out, leaving them alone.

They went out, and she looked across at him as he picked up their bags from the boot. 'How was Amelie when they left?'

He shrugged. 'A bit tearful, but she's been a lot happier this week, which is great. And next time, because Charlie's going to be here, they're just coming for the weekend and they'll take her out for days and bring her back.'

'And your mother?'

'She's home. Douglas brought her back.'

She studied his face. 'And?'

'Well, they were very circumspect, but there was a definite something going on. A sort of unspoken affection—but, you know, they've been friends for decades, and I'm probably just finding things that aren't there. So is that everything?'

'Yes, I think so,' she said, but his words were echoing in her head.

An unspoken affection.

Did people see that in them when she and Oliver looked at each other?

Did the children see it? This love between them that neither of them seemed able to acknowledge?

How long could they keep it up before it broke them? Because it felt like living in a house of cards, and the slightest breath of wind would bring it all crashing down around them.

They spent every evening together as a family, him, her, his mother and all the children, and every day was just bitter-sweet.

He came home every evening just after seven, and sometimes the children were still playing in the garden, busying themselves in the den or just running about giggling and letting off steam, and he'd grab them and scoop them up and hug them, sometimes ending up with all three at once, and the shrieks and giggles broke her heart.

He loved them all, and they loved him, but they were going nowhere, and it was tearing her in two.

They ended up together on the sofa every night after the children were in bed, and although she tried to keep her distance, it was difficult. Easier if Berry was lying in between them, but mostly she wasn't, and he'd hold out his arm and beckon her, and she'd end up snuggled against his side.

By the end of Thursday, she'd reached breaking-point. Oliver was heading to the airport in the morning, leaving at eight, so she did the Friday morning school run for them all as normal and went to work, then picked the children up and took them back to his to round up all their possessions.

The children ran in, and she found them all in the garden—Oliver, his mother and a young man almost the spitting image of his father when she'd met him.

Amelie was in her big brother's arms, her legs wrapped tightly round his waist, and he was laughing down at his little sister. And then he looked up and saw her crossing the lawn towards them, and he smiled his father's smile and her heart cracked in two.

'Hi. You must be Charlie,' she said, digging

out a smile from somewhere, and he freed a hand and held it out to her.

'And you must be Emily,' he said, his eyes searching hers as her hand was engulfed in a warm, confident grip. 'It's good to meet you. I've heard a lot about you.'

'All good, I hope,' she said lightly, and turned away, swamped with all sorts of might-have-beens. 'Billy, Phoebe, I'm just going to pack your stuff and then we're going home, OK?'

'Oh, Mummy, do we have to?' Phoebe asked, and Amelie said, 'Don't go! Why do you have to go? Charlie won't mind if you stay for the weekend.'

'But Charlie needs his room,' she pointed out, 'and anyway, we don't live here, sweet-heart.'

'But we sort of do,' Billy said, pleading, and she looked helplessly at Oliver.

'I'm going to pack. Maybe Oliver will get you all a drink while I do that.'

She headed back inside, blinking away tears, and ran upstairs to the room she'd been sleeping in. She'd packed her own things that morning before the children were up, and changed the sheets ready for Charlie, but the children's room was in chaos because Billy had unpacked his bag to find a different T-shirt before school, and half of Phoebe's things were missing. Hiding under the bed?

She had no idea, but she rounded up what she could, suddenly desperate to get away. Elizabeth didn't need her help with washing and dressing any more, and she really didn't know why she was still there. Maybe it was time to leave for good?

She was on her hands and knees on the bedroom floor when she heard his footsteps approaching.

'Lost something?'

My common sense? My heart...?

She got to her feet and stuffed the few things she'd found into Phoebe's bag. 'All sorts of somethings, but I dare say they'll turn up. I've stripped their beds, Charlie's room is ready for him, so I'm just going to head—'

'You don't have to, Emily. You could stay and eat with us, at least.'

She shook her head. 'No. Charlie's had a long day, and he'll need to rest, and I need to get the children settled back in.'

'Sunday, then. Come in time for supper. We can eat at five, if you like?'

She looked at him, then away again, her mind made up.

'No. I don't think so,' she said quietly, and

then made herself look back at him. 'You've got Charlie here now. You don't need me. Your mother's much better, she doesn't need my help with personal care now, and really, Amelie can get herself up and dressed quite easily, and your mother can walk her to school and back, and you can cook when you get home. If you batch cook while Charlie's here, you can freeze stuff so all you have to do is reheat it, and your mother can manage something simple for Amelie. You don't need me here any longer, Oliver. Not in any way.'

His face was confused, his eyes puzzled and hurt. 'That's not true. You know that's not true.' He reached out a hand and touched her cheek, and she flinched.

'Don't,' she said, and her voice cracked, and his face swam in front of her eyes.

'Em, what's going on? I don't understand.'

'Yes, you do. Us staying here was never supposed to be a long-term arrangement, and I don't think we should be seeing each other when Kath's here, either. It just makes it harder for us both and I can't do it any more.'

'No. No, Emily, don't do this to us, please.' His voice was raw with emotion, but she shook her head.

'I have to. The children are getting too

deeply into this. You heard them! And this situation with us, it's too fragile, too uncertain. I can't do it. I'm not ready, and neither are you, and in the meantime they're just getting in deeper and deeper, and so are we.'

She turned and met his eyes again, and they were filled with pain.

'We can do this, if we want it enough,' he said, but she shook her head, trying hard to stay strong, so near to weakening.

'No. No, we can't. We can't keep this in a compartment while I'm living with you, it's just not possible, and what we have outside of that isn't enough. It needs to be all or nothing, and it can't be all. There's too much at stake, and not just for us. We can't put the children through that again if it goes wrong.'

He reached out and wiped away her tears, his fingers infinitely gentle. 'We're older now, we know ourselves better, we know what matters. Why should it go wrong?'

'Because we're both rubbish at marriage, and the children don't deserve to be hurt again.' She stepped back, out of reach of that tender hand that she so wanted to lean into. 'Please, don't argue with me, Oliver. It's better this way.'

'Is it? It doesn't feel better. Not in any way,' he said gruffly, and he turned and walked away.

* * *

He watched them go, taking a huge chunk of his heart with them, and as he walked past the sitting room, he saw the chess set sitting on the side table, waiting for Billy's next move.

He walked over to it and stared down at the pieces. Billy was one move away from checkmate, but the boy hadn't realized.

He hadn't got the heart to put it away. He blinked hard and straightened up, and saw himself in the mirror above, his face raw with emotion.

Pull yourself together.

He sucked in a huge breath, let it out slowly and went back out into the garden to his family, but even though Charlie was there, he still felt that half his family was missing.

She held it together until she got into bed that night, but she hadn't changed the sheets since Oliver had been the week before, and she could still smell the faint, lingering scent of his cologne on the pillow.

Oh, Oliver...

She rolled her face into it and shed a river of silent tears for all they'd lost and all that might have been.

* * *

The next day was glorious, and the children wanted to go to the beach.

'I need to do a food order for tomorrow,' she said, but they begged and pleaded, so she scrabbled together a list for delivery the next morning, packed up the buckets and spades, the sun cream, the windbreak, the towels and spare clothes, and they set off for the short walk to the beach.

'Can we have an ice cream?' Billy asked, ever hungry, so she put everything down, dug out her card, paid for them, and they headed off again, with Billy in charge of hers as well as his.

They found a space on the beach, and she rescued what was left of her ice cream from her mischievous son and they sat down on the sand and ate them while she stared out over the sea and wondered how long it would take for the pain to go away.

For ever, she realized. It hadn't ever really gone from losing him the first time, and this time, somehow, felt even worse. Why had she let him back into her heart? Such a stupid thing to do—

'Are you all right, Mummy?'

She blinked hastily and smiled at Phoebe. 'Yes, darling, I'm fine. I've just got sun cream in my eye. Here, have a wet wipe. You've got ice cream all down your chin. Now, what about this sandcastle?'

'There's Billy and Phoebe!'

Damn. He might have known they'd be here today.

'Amelie, come back,' he called, but she was gone, running over the sand to join them.

'They're pretty tight, those kids,' Charlie said, giving him a look, and he let out a short, slightly broken sigh.

'Yes, they are. They've spent a lot of time together at ours because of Grandma, and they're at the same school, so they're bound to be close.'

'Hmm. Pity about you and Emily.'

'What about me and Emily?' he asked, trying to sound casual and wondering where on earth that had come from, but Charlie just raised an eyebrow.

'Uh—I do know about these things, Dad? I'm not a kid any more. And anyway, that's not what Grandma says. She agrees with me. She thinks it's a real shame she's gone.'

Damn. He looked away. 'You're all imagining it. There's nothing going on.' Not any more...

'So why do you look like someone's stolen your puppy?'

He ignored that and looked across at his daughter. 'I suppose we ought to go over there and retrieve her.'

'Well, good luck with that,' Charlie said with a wry laugh, because they were all down by the water's edge now, paddling ankle-deep as they scooped up water in buckets to bring back to the sandcastle moat that Emily was digging out a little farther up the beach.

As they headed towards her, she turned and glanced at them before looking away.

'Gorgeous day,' she said lightly, and carried on digging.

So they were down to talking about the weather. He would have laughed if he hadn't wanted to scream and cry.

'Need a hand?' he asked, and she started to say something when suddenly Charlie grabbed him.

'Billy's gone over in the water,' he said, and without thinking Oliver started to run.

'Where is he?'

'To your right—there.'

He saw a hand, way out, farther out than he'd imagined, and he kicked off his shoes and ran headlong into the surf, his heart in his mouth. He looked frantically around, but the hand was gone and there was no sign of him.

Please, no...

'Billy?' he yelled, ploughing through the waves, and as another one lifted and fell, he saw him briefly, but the beach was shelving sharply and he was suddenly out of his depth.

'Billy, I'm coming,' he yelled, powering through the surf, and then he was there, grabbing Billy by the arm and hauling him up out of the water against his chest.

'It's OK, Billy, I've got you,' he said, and as his feet found the bottom again and he stood up, the boy wrapped his arms and legs tightly round him and clung on.

He could feel the boy's chest heaving under his hand, but he had a horrible feeling he wasn't taking in any air.

Laryngospasm? It wasn't uncommon in drowning accidents, and if that was it, it would be short-lived. Please, God...

'Hey, Billy, it's OK. Just relax. You're safe now. It's all over,' he said, his voice soothing.

He waded out of the water, and as he reached Emily, he felt Billy suck in a huge lungful of air, and then he started to sob.

She plucked him out of Oliver's arms and sank down onto the wet sand with him, clinging to him and sobbing with relief, and Charlie came up to his father and put his arms round him and hugged him.

'Well done, Dad. That was pretty cool. I thought he was gone.'

He nodded. 'Yes, me, too, but it was your quick reaction that saved him. If you hadn't seen him...'

He hugged Charlie hard, then dropped down onto his knees by Emily, stroking a hand over Billy's sodden hair.

'Hey, little guy. How are you doing? You OK now?'

He nodded, his chest still heaving a bit but with sobs now, he thought.

Emily looked up at him, her eyes flooded with tears. 'I don't know how to thank you. I wasn't watching—'

'That was my fault. Charlie saw him. I wasn't watching, either. He had a bit of laryngospasm as I pulled him out, but I think he's OK now. Might be an idea to check him over.'

She nodded, burying her face in his skinny little shoulder and hugging him with a fierce tenderness that brought tears to Oliver's eyes.

If he hadn't found him under the water...

CHAPTER TEN

OLIVER HELPED HER to her feet, and they retreated to the prom and sat down on the edge of it, and he laid his ear against Billy's back and listened.

'It sounds OK. I think he might have got away with it. I need a stethoscope, really.'

She nodded. 'I've got one at home. I'll check him. Where's Phoebe?' she asked, her heart still racing, but she was just there, standing a few feet away with Amelie, and Charlie was squatting down, his arms around their shoulders, talking to them quietly. Reassuring them?

'Oh, Charlie,' she said, her eyes filling with tears again. 'Thank you so much. If you hadn't seen him…'

He shook his head, dismissing her thanks with a wave of his hand. 'Is he OK?'

'I think so, thanks to you and your father.' She looked up at Oliver. 'I need to take him home.'

'Yes, you probably do. Give me ten minutes. I'll go home and change and bring the car for you. Charlie, are you OK to stay with them all?'

He nodded. 'Sure. Here, I brought your shoes.'

He wasn't gone long, and by the time he got back the children were building the sandcastle again with Charlie's help, and Billy seemed fine.

She wasn't, far from it, but she wasn't surprised. She'd come so close to losing him...

Oliver had brought a stethoscope back with him, and he listened to Billy's chest all over, front and back.

'Is it OK?' she asked, and he nodded and handed the stethoscope to her as if he understood, and she checked him, too, just to reassure herself, knowing he would have done the same.

'Do you still want to go home?' he asked as Billy went back to his sandcastle, but she shook her head, the fear receding now Oliver was back and she knew Billy's chest was clear.

'No. I don't think so. He was scared, but he seems fine now and I don't really want to make it more than it was. But—could I hang on to this?' she asked, holding the stethoscope. 'Just in case?'

'Sure. If he's OK for the next hour or so and doesn't deteriorate, he's fine, but feel free to check if it reassures you.'

She smiled, but it was a feeble effort and her lips wobbled a bit. She firmed them and looked away, and he sat down next to her.

'Do you want me to stay?'

Yes, for ever...

'Do you think you need to?'

'Not for Billy, no. I think he's going to be fine, but you've had a heck of a scare.'

'I'm fine,' she lied. 'And actually, do you know what, it's getting really hot now. I might just take them home. Did you bring the car?'

He left Charlie to take Amelie home while he dropped Emily and the children off at her house, but he didn't go in. He hadn't been invited, for a start, and in any case there was an awkwardness between them that hadn't been there before she'd packed up and left him. No, not him, but his house. Subtle distinction that was pretty much lost on him.

He drove home, and by the time he got there Charlie and Amelie were back, telling his mother all about it.

She looked up at him, her eyes concerned.

'Is he all right?'

He nodded. 'Yes, he's fine.'

'And Emily?'

He looked away. 'She'll be OK. It was a bit of a shock.'

'Does she need you there?'

'No. She's got my number, and I'm sure she'll be keeping a very close eye on him.'

'It wasn't him I was worried about,' his mother said pointedly, but he wasn't prepared to get into this discussion again. It was none of their business and there was nothing he could do to change her mind.

'I'm going for a shower,' he said, and left them to it.

He was standing at the kitchen window, watching the last dying moments of the day when Charlie walked in and perched on a stool, his eyes thoughtful.

'You OK, Dad?'

'Yeah, I'm fine.'

'Are you really? You don't look it from where I'm sitting.'

He swallowed. 'I keep thinking about Billy,' he admitted gruffly. 'If you hadn't seen him get swept out—'

Charlie eyed him steadily. 'You love them, don't you? All of them.'

He looked away, and after a moment Charlie broke the stretching silence.

'I'll take that as a yes, then.'

He looked back at his son, wise beyond his years. 'It's…'

'Don't tell me it's complicated, Dad. It's always complicated. That's what we do, we complicate things, but really, it's simple. You love her, she loves you—what's holding you back?'

'We have—history.'

'I know that. Mom told me. She said you'd never stopped loving Emily, that that was part of what was wrong with your and Mom's relationship, and I guess it was part of what was wrong with you and Kath, too. Neither of them were Emily, and it's Emily that you love, that you've always loved. You and she were meant to be together.'

They were. Had Sue known that? Maybe. Not that it would have made any difference to their relationship ultimately, or to his and Kath's, because Charlie was right—it was Emily he wanted, Emily he loved.

'She doesn't trust me,' he said after an age. 'She daren't. I let her down before—which is how come you're here. And she daren't trust me or anyone else not to let her down again. It wasn't just me. Her husband left her, too, and went back to his first wife.'

'The woman he truly loved, I guess. Just like you love Emily. Go and tell her, Dad. Tell her you love her. Tell her you've always loved her.'

He had, but it had taken until now to realize it, even though it was staring him in the face. Was it really that simple? Maybe.

'If it helps, Grandma thinks you two should be together.'

He shot Charlie a keen look. 'How come you and Grandma think it's OK to discuss my private life?'

Charlie laughed, his eyes crinkling with affectionate amusement. 'What private life? You live in a family, Dad. You don't have a private life. Go. Go now, go and see her, tell her you love her, ask her to be with you. Give yourselves a chance.'

Could he? Did he dare lay his heart on the line?

'What if she says no?'

'What if she says yes? What if she *would* have said yes, but you never asked?'

He couldn't argue with that. Didn't want to. He shrugged away from the worktop, and Charlie slid off the stool and hugged him hard.

'Good luck. And don't hurry home. Amelie will be fine with me and Grandma. She loves Emily.'

'How do you know that?'

He smiled. 'Because she told me? She wants Emily to be her stepmother. And frankly, so do I.'

He blinked away sudden tears and gave Charlie a fierce hug. 'You'd better be right.'

'I'm always right. I love you. Now go.'

He walked round to her house, partly because it would give him time to think, and partly because if her lights were out he'd leave her in peace.

They weren't. There was a faint glow through her bedroom curtains, and the landing light was on. Was Billy in with her?

The downstairs was in darkness, and for an endless moment he hesitated, then he sent her a message.

Can I come in and talk to you?

She didn't respond at first, and he stood there on her drive, staring up at her bedroom window and feeling like a fool.

Of course she didn't want to talk to him. She'd made that quite clear—

Where are you?

Outside.

He saw the hall light come on, and the front door opened. She was wearing that silky robe again, her hair like a messy halo with the light behind her, and she sat on the step and waited as he walked towards her.

'How's Billy?'

'He's fine. You were right, it was just a temporary spasm, but he's been OK all day. He's asleep now.'

'And you?'

She stared at him, then looked away. 'I'm OK,' she said, but her voice was choked and he could tell she wasn't.

He went over to her and sat down, nudging her gently out of the way. 'He's OK, Em. It's all right.'

'I thought he was gone,' she said, her voice cracking, and he slid an arm around her shoulders and hugged her against his side.

'So did I.' He lifted a hand and wiped the tears off her cheeks, but she turned her head into his shoulder with a little sob, and he wrapped his arms around her and held her as she cried the tears that had been pending for hours.

'I don't know how to thank you. I owe you

so much. You saved his life,' she said brokenly, and he shook his head.

'You don't owe me anything. And anyway, it wasn't just me. Charlie saw him first, and there were dozens of people on the beach. Other people ran into the water.'

'But it was you who found him, you who saved him, you who knew how to calm him when he was terrified.' She looked up at him. 'And you're here now, just when I needed you. Maybe we should get married.'

'What, just because I rescued Billy? That's not a good enough reason, Emily, not when you still don't trust me.'

She shuffled away a fraction, and swiped the tears off her cheeks before she looked up at him searchingly.

'Why are you here, Oliver?'

Why, indeed. He took a slow breath, and let it out again. 'Because I knew you needed me, and I love you. I've always loved you, and I've never stopped loving you, and I never will.'

Her face contorted and she looked away, her chest heaving as she sucked in a breath. 'You don't know that.'

'I know I'll love you till the day I die,' he said honestly. 'Look me in the eye and tell me you don't love me.'

She slowly turned her head to look at him,

and in the light from the hall he could see tears glistening in her eyes.

'I can't.'

'Can't what? Can't love me? Or can't tell me that you love me?'

She gave a shaky sigh. 'I've always loved you, Oliver, and I've never dared to let myself love anyone again, not really, but you're right, I daren't trust you. It didn't work last time, and what if it goes wrong again? What if I move in with you properly and it all falls apart?'

'Why would it? Unless we neglect it. All marriages, all relationships take work. My parents used to argue all the time, but they always worked through it, and they loved each other to the end.'

He took her hand and pressed a kiss to her cold, lifeless fingers. 'I love you, Emily, and I want to be with you for the rest of my life. Don't do this to us. Give us a chance, please.'

'And what if it goes wrong? What if the children fall out?'

'Children always fall out, but they get over it. You know that. It's all part of growing up. And you saw them yesterday. They didn't want to go, and Amelie didn't want you to go. And today, Amelie was so excited to see them on the beach, and so worried about Billy. I was, too. That's why I came here tonight, because he's all I've been able to think about all day. I love him. Emily. I love you all, and we need to be together, for all our sakes.'

He did love them all.

She knew that, deep down in her heart. He'd been wonderful with the children, and they'd loved being a part of his family. Was she just being a coward?

'I'm scared,' she said, her voice a little unsteady. 'I'm scared to love you. It means too much, and if I let it in, and it goes away again—'

'It won't. I won't. I'll never leave you. I know you don't feel you can trust me, but I'd rather cut my own heart out than leave you ever again. Marry me, Emily. Come back to me. I need you. We all need you. Please, give me another chance. Give us a chance.'

She searched his eyes, raw with emotion, filled with sincerity, gleaming with unshed tears.

One slipped down his cheek, and she reached out a finger and wiped it gently away.

I'd rather cut my own heart out than leave you ever again...

'Are you sure?'

He laughed, but it cracked in the middle. 'Yes, I'm sure. I've never been more sure of anything in my life. And yes, it's complicated, yes, it might be tricky from time to time, yes, it'll be a juggling act, but there'll be two of us to catch it if we drop the ball, and we can do this. We can do it together, if you can find the courage to believe in us.'

She held her breath for an age, then let it out and smiled at him as the tears started to spill down her cheeks. 'Yes,' she said, and then just to be sure, she said it again.

'Yes, yes, I love you. Yes, I'll marry you. And please don't cut your heart out. That would be so messy.'

He gave a choked laugh and pulled her into his arms, and they clung to each other for the longest time. And then he let her go and reached into the pocket of his jeans, pulling out something small.

'I don't know if this'll still fit you. I bought it before I went to America, but I never got a chance to give it to you.'

He held it out to her on the palm of his hand, a simple gold ring with a little row of diamonds, and she picked it up and stared down at it, her eyes welling with tears. The diamonds sparkled as they caught the light, and she handed it to him and held out her ring finger.

'Only one way to find out,' she said with a smile, and he slid it onto her finger. She stared at it through the mist of tears. 'I can't believe you've had it all this time.'

He smiled ruefully. 'I couldn't bring myself to get rid of it. Maybe I just never gave up hope. I'll get you a better one.'

'No. I don't want a better one, I want this one, because it has far more meaning than a new one could ever have.'

She swallowed the sudden lump in her throat and, lifting her head, she leaned across and kissed him fleetingly, then stood up and pulled him to his feet.

'Come to bed, my love,' she murmured, and he followed her in through the door.

He sent Charlie a text at six the next morning, and a moment later he got a rude but heartfelt reply that made him laugh.

Emily looked at him sleepily. 'What is it?'

'Charlie. I think he's happy for us,' he said, his arm round her and her head resting on his shoulder. 'We need to go and see them.'

'We do,' she said. 'How will Amelie be? Do you need to talk to her before we tell mine?'

He laughed. 'I don't think so. She told Charlie she wants you to be her stepmother.'

Her eyes widened, and a slow smile bloomed on her face. 'Really?'

'Really. Did you sleep?'

'Off and on. I checked on Billy a few times.'

'I thought you did—ah, I can hear the children. Do you want me to get dressed?'

Too late. The door opened, and Billy and Phoebe came in, stopped dead and then threw themselves at him.

'You're here!' Billy said, and snuggled up against his chest, and as he wrapped his arms around the boy he was swamped with emotion.

If he hadn't been there, if he hadn't found him... Not now.

'Yeah. Mummy's got something to ask you.'

He sat up and they looked at Emily, and she smiled. 'You know you wanted to live with Amelie and Oliver and Grandma? Did you mean that?'

They nodded. 'Are we going to? For ever?' Phoebe asked, eyes widening.

'If that's what you want?'

They leaped up and started bouncing on the bed, and Oliver laughed.

'We'll take that as a yes. Maybe we should go and tell the others?'

They found them in the kitchen—Charlie, Amelie, his mother and of course Berry, who leaped up to greet them.

Amelie's eyes lit up. 'Have you come for

breakfast?' she asked Emily, and Oliver gave a strangled laugh.

'Well, yes, but—you know you said you wanted Billy and Phoebe to stay here? Well, how would you feel if Emily and I got married and they all came back to live with us for ever?'

Her eyes widened. 'For ever?' she shrieked, and threw herself at him, hugging him hard. 'That would be the best thing *ever*!' she said, and they all ran out into the garden, taking Berry with them.

He turned and met his mother's eyes, and there was something in them he couldn't quite read.

'Congratulations,' she said softly. 'I'm so glad you've both finally come to your senses.'

'We've both made too many mistakes to do anything rash, Mum. We needed to take our time, and we've done that. This is permanent. This is for ever.'

'Good,' she said, and then went on carefully, 'does that mean you no longer need me?'

'Mum, you'll always have a home here—'

'But what if I don't want it? What if there's somewhere else I'd rather be?'

He searched her eyes, and he felt the smile start from way down inside him. 'Douglas,' he said gently, and she nodded.

'I wouldn't abandon you, I'll always be here to help out, and we'll take it slowly, but we want to be together.'

'You're not rushing this?'

She laughed. 'Darling, I'm nearly seventy, Douglas is seventy-one. Unlike you two, we don't have the luxury of procrastination. And anyway, I've known him since before you were born. It's hardly hasty.'

She was right, and he was just so happy for her.

'Come here,' he said, and hugged her hard. When he turned round, Charlie was hugging Emily, and there were tears in her eyes.

'Come here, you two,' he said, holding out his arm to them, and she and Charlie moved into the hug.

Three generations, two families, one great big happy ending.

Finally...

EPILOGUE

THEY HAD A simple family wedding.

Not a quiet wedding, not with all the children there, but simple and heartfelt, followed by a garden party back at Oliver's house.

No. Their house, the house where they were living now and would continue to live.

Charlie was his best man, of course, and he insisted on making a speech which had everyone in stitches. And then in tears.

'You've waited too long for this moment,' he said, suddenly serious, his voice cracking. 'I don't think I've ever met anyone who deserved their happy ending more than you two, and I couldn't be happier for you—for all of you. For all of us. For the children, for the whole family, but most of all for you two. I love you. Everyone, please raise your glasses for the bride and groom!'

'The bride and groom!' they chorused, and Emily turned to look at Oliver, his eyes filled

254 FINDING THEIR FOREVER FAMILY

with tears as he wrapped his arms around her and kissed her tenderly.

Then he turned to his extended family with a slightly crooked smile, his arm still around her shoulders, holding her firmly against his side.

'Relax, guys. I'm not going to make a speech, mostly because I don't think I'd get through it, but I do just need to thank Mum for all the support she's given me, the children for all we've put them through, and most of all I need to thank Emily for giving me another chance, and making me the happiest man alive. I love you, Em. Always have, always will, and that's a promise.'

'I love you, too,' she said, her own voice breaking, and as she went back into his arms, their whole family crowded round them for a massive group hug.

'What a wonderful day.'

'It is. The best day.'

Oliver put his arm round her, and she rested her head on his shoulder with a quiet sigh. He glanced down at her. 'You OK?'

'Very OK. You?'

'Never better. It's just so great to see everyone we love together. I can't believe how well they all get on.'

They did. Their mothers were sitting together on the bench smiling and laughing and getting to know each other, Berry at their feet, and Douglas and her father were standing watching the children play doctors and nurses while Charlie lay on the grass being a very patient patient and hamming it up.

'We feel like a proper family,' she said softly, and she felt his lips press against her hair.

'We are. At last. It's the end of a long, long road.'

'And look where it's brought us. Four wonderful children that would never have existed if we hadn't travelled it.' She turned to face him. 'Did I ever tell you how much I love you?'

His lips twitched. 'I'm not sure. Maybe you'd better do it again.'

'I love you. I love you I love you I love you. Better?'

'Much better.' His eyes were suddenly serious, the smile gone, and he cupped her face in his hands, his fingers oh-so gentle, and as he lowered his head, he murmured, 'I love you, too, so much. And I'm so, so sorry that I hurt you, but I'm here now, and I'm staying, and I love you. I'll always love you—now and for ever...'

His lips met hers, and in the background

they could hear a chorus of cheers and catcalls. She felt him smile before he lifted his head and winked at her, then he turned, his arm still round her, and led her back to the others.

Back to their forever family...

* * * * *

If you enjoyed this story, check out these other great reads from Caroline Anderson

The Midwife's Miracle Twins
Healing Her Emergency Doc
Tempted by the Single Mom
From Heartache to Forever

All available now!